Entreplexity® = Entɪ
Complexɪty

Critical Issues in the Future of Learning and Teaching
Volume No 9

This series represents a forum for important issues that do and will affect how learning and teaching are thought about and practised. All educational venues and situations are undergoing change because of information and communications technology, globalization and paradigmatic shifts in determining what knowledge is valued. Our scope includes matters in primary, secondary and tertiary education as well as community-based informal circumstances. Important and significant differences between information and knowledge represent a departure from traditional educational offerings heightening the need for further and deeper understanding of the implications such opportunities have for influencing what happens in schools, colleges and universities around the globe. An inclusive approach helps attend to important current and future issues related to learners, teachers and the variety of cultures and venues in which educational efforts occur. We invite forward-looking contributions that reflect an international comparative perspective illustrating similarities and differences in situations, problems, solutions and outcomes.

Edited by Michael Kompf (michael.kompf@brocku.ca - Brock University, Canada) & Pamela M. Denicolo (p.m.denicolo@reading.ac.uk - University of Reading, UK)

Michael Kompf is Professor of Education at Brock University, Canada. Interests include developmental issues for adult learners and teachers; personal construct psychology; global policies and practices in higher education; and philosophies of inquiry. Recent writing and presentations have included exploring the nature of university corporatism, higher education success rates, individual and the social implications of distance learning, and Aboriginal education. A member of the International Study Association on Teachers and Teaching (isatt.org) since 1985, Michael has served four terms as Chair in addition to four terms as editor of the ISATT Newsletter. Michael is a member of several professional associations and serves as associate editor and reviewer on several journals. He is co-editor of six volumes of work in adult education and the various areas of teacher thinking. He has consulted, presented papers and given lectures throughout North America, the EU and Australasia.

Pam M. Denicolo is the Director of the Graduate School at the University of Reading and an active member of the University Committee for Postgraduate Research Studies. Her passion for supporting and developing graduate students is also demonstrated through her contributions to the UK

Council for Graduate Education Executive Committee, the Society for Research into Higher Education Postgraduate Network, and other national and international committees and working groups which, for example, review and evaluate research generic skills training and the concordance of UK universities with the European Code and Charter, produce a framework of skills for researchers over their full career and consider the changing nature of the doctorate. As a psychologist working particularly in the fields of Professional and Postgraduate Education, she has supervised more than 50 doctoral students to successful completion, examined many more, and developed and led Research Methods Programmes for social scientists in her current and previous universities. She was honoured to be appointed an Honorary Member of the Royal Pharmaceutical Society for her contributions to the education of pharmacists. Her lifelong interest in student learning, and hence teachers' teaching, led her to become an active member of the International Study Association on Teachers and Teaching (ISATT) and serving member of the Executive Committee for many years. Her research has been oriented by a commitment to understanding the way participants in learning processes construe their roles, situations and activities, through the use and development of Personal Construct Theory approaches and methods.

Entreplexity® = Entrepreneurship + Complexity:

The Writing and Thoughts of Gene Luczkiw

Michael Kompf
Brock University, Ontario, Canada

SENSE PUBLISHERS
ROTTERDAM / TAIPEI

A C.I.P. record for this book is available from the Library of Congress.

ISBN: 978-94-6209-062-0 (paperback)
ISBN: 978-94-6209-063-7 (hardback)
ISBN: 978-94-6209-064-4 (e-book)

Published by: Sense Publishers,
P.O. Box 21858,
3001 AW Rotterdam
The Netherlands
https://www.sensepublishers.com

Printed on acid-free paper

TABLE OF CONTENTS

Section Three: Exercises and Applications

Section Four: *Colleagues' Responses to Entreplexity® = Entrepreneurship + Complexity*

FOREWORD

Gene Luczkiw was instinctively an innovator and a visionary whose keen intellect, natural curiosity, enthusiasm and optimism inspired anyone he came in contact with be it locally, nationally or globally, whether through teaching, mentoring, consulting or collaborating with others. I know this about Gene as I was married to him for over 30 years, having initially met him as a colleague at McArthur College of Education, Queen's University in Kingston, Ontario. In addition, I worked alongside Gene as a facilitator at the Institute for Enterprise Education (IEE) in St. Catharines, Ontario, Canada, which he founded in the early 90s, as well as in the Bachelor of Education, Enterprise Education Program at Brock University, St. Catharines, Ontario, of which IEE was a partner.

In the late 20th century, when manufacturing sectors were beginning to be decimated in Niagara and North America, Gene recognized that people were facing a very different career future from what they had been raised to expect. His strong belief in humanity and its ability to change placed him on a road similar to Asterope, whom he cites in the second part of this book.

Gene concluded that for people to succeed in this new world order it was necessary to create an enterprising culture, hence he commenced down a path to understand what it meant to be 'enterprising'. He researched over 2200 entrepreneurs worldwide to discover what made them 'tick' and, from his findings, emerged an intriguing set of characteristics that many of them shared. Recognizing that very few people were capable of becoming entrepreneurs in the true sense of the word, he did, however, feel that most people could become enterprising, based on the entrepreneurial attributes that he uncovered in his research. This led him into many areas of interest, including the Science of Complexity, where he often found answers to questions that kept popping up in his research.

As he reflected on these many subjects and areas of interest, Gene loved to pen his thoughts on them, and often his writings appeared in the many models and courses that he developed and delivered over the years. Those fortunate enough to have had him as a speaker, facilitator or educator will recognize some of his ideas and conclusions that appear in this book.

Dr. Michael Kompf, the editor of this book, was a great friend, colleague and mentor of Gene. I sincerely want to thank Michael for reviewing Gene's writings and editing some of them into this first book - Entreplexity® = Entrepreneurship + Complexity. It is a real tribute to Gene, and to me, to keep his spirit alive. Needless to say, Gene's passing was not only a huge loss for me, but for anyone who knew him. Gene wanted to live forever as he had so much work he wanted to accomplish. His passion was to help people find their true meaning and purpose in life.

Jane Luczkiw
St. Catharines, Ontario
Canada
2012

BIOGRAPHY OF GENE LUCZKIW

Gene Luczkiw was a recognized global expert in the fields of entrepreneurship development, entrepreneurial leadership and enterprise education. Gene was both an academic and a practitioner in the field and consulted with some of the world's largest public and private organizations. Gene was the founding director of both the Institute for Enterprise Education (IEE) and the Centre for Global Innovation and Leadership (CGIL). IEE was an international centre dedicated to the research, design and development of training in the fields of entrepreneurship, entrepreneurial leadership and enterprise education. CGIL was dedicated to the transformation of existing organizations in both the private and public sectors into entrepreneurial entities.

Gene's professional activities focused on entrepreneurial research and innovative program design dedicated to the creation of entrepreneurs and enterprising individuals. Among Gene's leading-edge innovations were methodologies that empower individuals and leaders to break out of existing 'mental models' in order to create new possibilities and identify new opportunities, while exploiting emerging niches in today's chaotic, complex and discontinuous global environment. The *seven determinants of successful enterprises* model has become the model of choice among leading organizations around the globe.

In the academic field, Gene served as an adjunct professor in the Faculty of Education at Brock University. Gene was responsible for pioneering a number of undergraduate courses at the Faculty of Business at Brock University, as well as, co-developing a specialist certificate in entrepreneurship education at the Faculty of Education at Brock University.

One of Gene's pioneering efforts was the development of the Bachelor of Education, Enterprise Education Program in partnership with IEE and Brock University's Faculty of Education. This innovative program for pre-service secondary teachers focused upon linking teacher education with enterprise education by enabling learners to discover their distinct strengths and talents as the necessary first step of the learning journey. This program also enabled learners to link their strengths with opportunities in the workplace environment as part of the teaching and learning process.

Gene's consulting activities included the EINET (European Union partnership for enterprise education and training in Europe); Organisation for economic co-operation and development (OECD); World Bank, Washington, D.C.; RBC Royal Bank; Scottish Enterprise, U.K.; London life; the Coca-Cola company, North America; Canadian Broadcasting Corporation; Johnson & Johnson, U.S.A.; Government of Canada; the Woodbridge group; Managing Directors' Academy, Oulu, Finland; Bell Canada; Henry of Pelham Family Estate Winery; Automotive Parts Manufacturers' Association; The Institute for Management Studies; Ontario's cabinet office's Centre for Leadership; Verdant Power Canada (Chairman of the board).

Gene was honoured as a finalist in the supporter of entrepreneurship category in Ernst & Young's entrepreneur of the year awards (Ontario, Canada) in 1995 and again, in 1997. Gene was the recipient of the 2004 Hillmer award for honorary life membership in the Ontario Business Educators' Association. In 2005, Gene was named a senior fellow at the University of Essex (U.K.) Centre for Entrepreneurship, Innovation and Management. Gene also co-authored an entrepreneurship text, *Creativity in business – an entrepreneurial approach* (1992). In 2002, Gene was awarded the Queen Elizabeth II Golden Jubilee medal for his commitment and service to the community and to Canada.

> *Gene's mission was: "to change the world by enabling people to develop enterprising and innovative habits to meet the challenges of the knowledge age."*

INTRODUCTION

Do not go where the path may lead, go instead where there is
no path and leave a trail.

Ralph Waldo Emerson

It has taken longer than expected to put together a volume of work that gives fair representation to Gene (Eugene) Luczkiw. Gene was a friend, colleague, collaborator, mentor, fellow learner and one of the most unique and irrepressible characters I have ever met. Sitting down with him for whatever purpose was never just a meeting, it was an encounter. Elegant pen in hand, he would take notes until a shiny new idea flew through his processes and clicked with books he had read, someone he met and talked with, something he had heard on the radio, which in turn reminded him of a story he heard, or an experience he had while here, there or some other place. Gesticulating wildly, Gene's arms, hands and often his entire body conducted a symphony of ideas while he spoke or listened displaying his excitement in meeting and talking with a wide a range of individuals. Gene learned something from everyone.

Gene's ideas and connections led to the formulation of Entreplexity® – his word for the complex face of entrepreneurial thought. Gene often discussed what word other than entrepreneurship would convey the meaning of enterprising thought because *entrepreneurship* seemed to be one of those tagged words that had a slightly negative semantic connotation in some circles... especially in the academy of the day. His goal was to understand and retool the connections individuals had with their lives and experiences, enabling them to repurpose whatever social, academic and intellectual baggage they carried to their best advantage. To this end, Gene studied entrepreneurs less for achieved stature and success and more for the thought processes and persistence that brought them through failure and frustration.

Gene Luczkiw was contagion of curiosity. He addressed his own questions and with the twist of a word or idea showed a creative dexterity that infected all those in his world. His professional and academic life cast him as a crusader for personal empowerment through teaching individuals to assume responsibility for their own life and to act in ways that were beneficial to themselves and others. He accomplished this and found ways to touch the lives of all he encountered.

How then to present Gene's work in a way that illustrated his many sides? I was fortunate to have access to his many boxes of papers, saved documents and some of the academic work he produced during his graduate studies. A short version of the major research paper produced in completion of his Master of Education degree is presented in the first part of this volume. This work was finalized, submitted and accepted in the short year before Gene's passing and is likely the final work he produced. In this piece Gene's voice comes through and shows a marked contrast in style compared with the background writing that follows. In many respects, it is the summary piece that represents much of what he attempted to accomplish. A mixture of triumph and irony shows as the success of his program measured by individual accomplishments meant most to Gene.

The second part of this book provides a deep and thoughtful grasp of academic and business theory grounding Gene's approach to learning, teaching and life, in general. In this section, Gene shows the breadth of what he read, studied, thought about and connected. The third section contains a number of activities, exercises and information that provide practical applications for enterprise education. The fourth section contains commentaries sent by friends and colleagues of Gene's who were of great assistance in reading an early draft of this manuscript. Readers will note that different reference styles are used in Sections One and Two. Section One was written using APA style as required in the Social Sciences. Section Two uses a Chicago-style reference format with which Gene was more familiar.

Acknowledgements are made to Jane Luczkiw for her gracious patience and support; to Lisa Cairns for providing electronic copies of Gene's work and her activities in keeping his message alive. Thanks to Patrick Tierney for formatting and patience as well. Errors and omissions are mine, the brilliance belongs to the "Motivator".

Thanks Gene.
Michael Kompf, August 2012

PS During a phone call with Jane Luczkiw while doing final edits, she told me that she had found a written note among Gene's papers and wondered if I thought it could or should be included. While the reader will ultimately judge, I can't think of a better way to start off.

A note found on Gene's desk:

From my early years as a child, I have always yearned to discover answers to the following questions:

- Why do I exist?
- How did I get here?
- What is it that I should be doing?
- How do I know what to do?

In 7th grade, my elementary school principal, Bill Olesevich, dubbed me the 'friendly philosopher'. From my humble beginnings on a mixed-use farm, I had ample opportunity as an only child to reflect upon these questions. Little did I know at that time that by pursuing answers to these questions, I was developing my conscious side. Needless to say, after many years of attempting to make sense of my existence, meaning and purpose in life, I discovered my mission: 'To enable people to discover their purpose in life.' Over the past two decades, I have worked with thousands of individuals in business, education and government in an effort to share my research and practical experiences.

This paper is the culmination of this work. Perhaps you have been on a similar journey, often interrupted by daily routines both at home and in the workplace. In most cases, I have found people to be driven either by their genetic blueprint, their cultural rules or a combination of the above two. Rarely, have they stopped to reflect upon their actions. They just did it!

If you are seeking a greater understanding of the forces at work in your lives and how you can harness them to do your bidding, this book is for you.

So, let's begin by looking first at the how's and why's of our existence and then develop strategies to create our future. On your mark, ready, fire, aim.

A PRACTICE IN SEARCH OF A THEORY

(From an early draft of Gene's M.Ed. major research project)

This major research project is the culmination of my personal and professional journey into the field of teacher education. It begins with my teaching career some 35 years ago and my own development a practitioner and researcher. The autobiographic approach I have taken presents the reader with an alternate approach to teaching and learning that has been my trademark from my very first day in the classroom. For many years, however, I relied on my intuition to guide me through the challenging landscape, serving me well along the way.

In the early '90s, I became engaged in action-based research, in order to develop effective models that could be replicated by others seeking an alternative teaching and learning experience. During my career, I have always been a learner, first, and facilitator of learning, second. The challenges I faced in the university environment, especially at the Faculty of Business, strengthened my resolve to develop models for teaching and learning that would encapsulate my professional practice and share it with those who chose a career in teaching.

It was meeting Dr. Michael Kompf in the late '90s that presented me with a coach and mentor who would guide me through the turbulence of learning, to complete the Master of Education program at Brock. Thanks to Dr. Kompf's wisdom, I have finally been able to share my journey with those who may seek to move to a beat of a different drummer.

THE MEANING OF ENTERPRISE: THE TEACHERS' PERSPECTIVES

Three themes emerge when the definitions of enterprise proposed by graduates of the Bachelor of Education, Enterprise Education program are clustered. The three themes include self-motivation, goal driven and networker. By self-motivated, graduates talk of the need to understand oneself and to enable students to discover their strengths, talents, motivation and creativity. I call these the three C's – contribution, commitment and creativity. Goal driven that the graduates propose means that the teacher's goals should fit into the school's vision if one even exists. They recognize that to grasp opportunities, teachers need to be flexible and adaptable to change and take advantage of using innovative approaches in the classroom. The importance of networking can never be overstated. The teacher seeks to work collaboratively with colleagues and the larger school community. By bringing the living community into the classroom, students will be afforded alternate ways of using their contribution, commitment and creativity. They will become enterprising.

As an enterprising teacher, my goal is to assist students find their true selves, and in doing so, evoke an awareness of their ethic and morals which differentiates them from others. As an enterprising teacher, I strive to teach, as well as learn from my students, in an open and collaborative environment.

As an enterprising teacher, I look beyond the ordinary in a quest to bring the world into the classroom and to provide an authentic, meaningful environment in which each individual will thrive and achieve personal success. An enterprising teacher is an innovative and reflective practitioner with a demonstrated commitment to lifelong learning. She/He values the learner as a person with unique talents, experiences and insights. She/He strives to engage her/his students in learning by using authentic and well-planned learning activities, humour and innovative approaches to achieve that goal. She/He espouses the value of collaboration and demonstrates it by maintaining a network of community members and colleagues.

A PRACTICE IN SEARCH OF MY OWN THEORY

For as long as I can remember, I always enjoyed deconstructing things and then putting them together in a different manner. In my adolescent years, I was considered different because I tended to live in the future. In the seventh grade, I was dubbed the 'friendly philosopher' by my principal and teacher. To me 'anything is possible' and if someone were to say 'that's impossible', I would immediately retort with the opposite response.

Armed with this belief system, I continued to face uphill challenges throughout my educational journey. I recall being called to the office of my high school principal. I had just written the Scholastic Aptitude Tests – Ontario (SATO), based on the U.S. Scholastic Aptitude Tests (SAT), in math and science. He wanted to know why I was almost failing these courses. I said they were not a challenge for me. He asked me to change my mind. When I reached Grade 13, I dropped both maths and the science course. I was more interested in history where I didn't seem to have the aptitude, but certainly had the attitude and the marks that go with it. I suppose I liked a challenge.

After graduating from university with majors in political science and economics, I decided to go to law school to pursue the next leg of my learning journey. Unfortunately, an unanticipated event took place. My father, who was my source of income support, died suddenly and, being the only child in the family, I was vested with taking care of my mother and the small estate my father left. It was also a pivotal time in my life. Although I enjoyed the academic discipline of law, I was not keen in its practical application. I asked for a year's leave of absence and went about settling the estate. I was fairly certain that I would not return.During this year, I met a friend who advised me to consider teaching as a career. It would only take me one year to get a degree and jobs were readily available.

Based on my experiences with excellent high school teachers and some superb professors at university, I decided to give it a shot. I enrolled in the Business

Education Program at the Faculty of Education, University of Toronto. I enjoyed teachers' college and, for the first time, I was free to use my creative juices. I started developing eight millimetre films on various aspects of marketing. This did not go unnoticed by my marketing professor, Bruce Conchie, who somehow managed to find me placements where I could put my creative juices to work. Needless to say, I had found my niche in life.

I was fortunate to teach in two open concept schools, both products of the Hall-Dennis Report. Public education in Ontario had been influenced by this 1968 report that recommended a student-centred approach for teaching and learning. As a result of the Hall-Dennis report, educational guidelines in the province of Ontario called for increased student autonomy and less teacher direction. The key decision makers were aware that while this approach might work for some students, it would not work for others. Although the report had the best of intentions in mind, a lot was left to uninitiated teachers and administrators. A small number of educators were enthusiastic about the prospects of using a variety of approaches that would be used depending upon the students' learning styles, as opposed to an unstructured student-centred approach.

A.Y. Jackson in North York, Ontario was my first school. The conditions and culture of this handpicked staff were such that, in my rookie season, I felt I had been there for years. It was at A. Y. Jackson that I began designing various simulations and experiential activities that would engage students in learning activities. I had long discovered that traditional teaching methods would not work for me. I would rather begin working in a messy situation with my class and gently guide them to create order out of chaos. In addition, these students came from high-powered families and this enabled us to visit their parents' workplaces. This included attending a commercial being shot at CTV (a Canadian television network), as well as a Shoppers Drugmart buyers' market, to name a few. The outside world rapidly became a classroom for both learner and teacher.

During my early teaching career, I spent a great deal of time getting to know each of my students in order to get a sense of their needs as individuals. Many of these needs had nothing to do with the classroom itself. By being a good listener, however, and by creating a safe and respectful environment, I was able to get their attention. I also discovered that if I wanted their ongoing attention I could not make learning merely transmission of knowledge. I had not read Hart (2001) at the time, but he described that teaching for wisdom meant constantly asking who we are and who we are becoming. In addition, I needed to know what the learners enjoyed doing for its own sake, and how this could be transported into a learning situation.

I learned from courses taught by Dr. Michael Kompf in the Master of Education program at Brock that the theme related to beginning with ourselves is based on George Kelly's belief that every person is his/her own psychologist. Psychology is the study of human affairs and every one of us has a wealth of knowledge based on our experiences. New ideas and theories grow from personal experiences and provide a rich source of knowledge about human affairs. By beginning with yourself, you are taking advantage of tapping into what you know about yourself and others. Psychologists call these interpersonal relations. These include self-awareness, individual differences, teaching and learning.

Hunt (1987), working with teachers, discovered a variation of teaching styles that adapt to the special needs of students. Working at schools, such as Thornlea, Hunt became more dissatisfied with the idea that 'theory leads to practice'. It did not adequately describe how we, as people, work together. Hunt found that this approach removed the realities of the practice we sought to improve. According to Hunt (1987, p. 5) 'there is nothing so theoretical as good practice'. Hunt introduced the inside-out and outside-in approaches to teaching and learning. Inside-out psychology is rooted in your own experience. The outside-in psychology defers human affairs to external experts. According to Hunt, we have been brainwashed to believe that the experts hold the knowledge about human affairs. As teachers, for example, we need to get out of this paradigm. Hunt identifies three significant benefits of beginning with ourselves using the inside-out process: It enhances our understanding of who we are, improves our ability to communicate with others and provides the necessary framework for changing out actions.

Hunt relies upon the Conceptual Learning Model (CLM). He designed this model to improve the educational experience of inner city, disadvantaged youth, much like our Youth Enterprise Program at IEE, which I developed for at-risk learners. The idea of the CLM model rests upon the idea of matching one's teaching approach to the needs of the learner, by linking the learner's conceptual level with the appropriate degree of structure.

The principle is based on the notion that the degree of structure in the learning environment should complement the student's need for it. A good example was my experience with a student at A.Y.Jackson school in my early years of teaching. He had committed many criminal acts as a juvenile. Most of his issue was not getting enough attention in the home environment. When time came for me to teach about the Juvenile Delinquency Act, he proudly strolled to the front of the class and proceeded to describe the purpose of the act and then engaged students in a question and answer session. With only a few details to fill in, I was able to attribute the success of the unit to that student.

I began to ask the question "Why should we begin with ourselves". I began to listen to my students' stories during the course of my classroom experience. They began to share their experiences and in the process, I began to get a read on their strengths and talents, by the use of experiential activities that helped me see what they brought with them to class each day.

I would later develop a more detailed framework for storytelling on behalf of my students. I started putting them in diverse groups, based on the nature of their contribution and motivation, to perform certain activities.

Reflecting upon these experiences, I soon discovered that once learners were provided with a safe environment where everyone would be treated with respect, they would also learn to know, learn to do and learn to live together (Delors, 1996). These three pillars operated in a non-linear fashion depending upon the nature of the challenge faced by the groups. Later, these experiences at both secondary schools that I taught in would be influential in developing two themes for teaching and learning. In fact, these two themes could be expanded into the private and public sector organizations: The need to create conditions and cultures that enabled each person to connect his/her distinct talents, motivation and creativity with meaningful work, and the need to discover one's contribution, commitment and creativity. These two factors would become the essential framework for teaching and learning within the Bachelor of Education, Enterprise Education program at Brock.

I was able to create conditions and cultures for learning because I, myself, worked in such an environment, at least in the early stages at A.Y.Jackson, and later stages, at Governor Simcoe. Greenleaf (1977) contrasts two different kinds of leaders that shape the nature and quality of their environments. One type of leader is driven by power and/or monetary rewards, focusing on his/her personal and professional growth, usually at the expense of those they lead. Unlike the Lone Ranger, as described by Sergiovanni (1992), the other type of leader is first and foremost, a servant. The question Greenleaf posits is: Do those who are served grow as individuals personally and professionally? An example of servant leadership in schools takes place when teachers are motivated, not by bureaucratic rules and regulations, but by the importance of helping learners discover their place in their respective community. It was within this type of environment that I felt free to create my own distinct classroom environment to pursue my mission: To enable each person to discover their essence of being and share this with others in their community.

It is this mission that compelled me to search for methods to engage my students in a learning journey. As already mentioned, one of my early innovations was to create simulation games as a means of learning about a particular subject. Although it took time to create these games, they could be immediately tested in the classroom environment. Imagine the challenges that I faced when some of the students were grasping the outcomes of the game, before I had a chance to add another complication to it. While these games worked for some of my students, there was still a major element missing. I usually had my students pick their own groups, rather than me having any input into the selection process. I came to the realization that every person's learning style was, indeed, distinct from one another. This was the result of their distinct cognitive intelligence, as well as their emotional intelligence. It would be later that I would learn about Howard Gardner's *Multiple Intelligences* (1983) and Goleman's (1998) *Emotional Intelligence*.

Hunt (1987) pointed out that while cognition is well developed in most teens, it is their emotional state that leads to immature behaviour in both their personal and social lives. It appears the various interactive activities increased their levels of emotional maturity. Later, I would discover why when I studied the work of psychologist Mihaly Csikszentmihalyi (1990).

In the spring of 1976, I was asked to teach marketing and related business subjects at McArthur College of Education, Queen's University in Kingston, Ontario. That was the summer that I met my future wife, Jane, who was also asked to teach Business Education subjects at McArthur, as well. There was a third factor in 1976. I had decided to leave A.Y. Jackson in the spring. With the arrival of a new principal and the putting up of walls everywhere, the original open concept began to lose its lustre in the eyes of the North York Board of Education. In fact, many of the original teachers began to be moved to other schools. The experiment with open concept had come to a rapid end.

Governor Simcoe School in St. Catharines was originally an open concept school, as well. Its principal, Bob Hayes, had also handpicked his staff and had replicated many of the good things that took place at one time at A. Y. Jackson. Unfortunately a year after my arrival at Simcoe, Bob Hayes retired.

An administrator was brought in to put an end to the open concept idea with a shared decision-making model. This model's practical approach was he would make the decisions and we would have to follow them. Fortunately, I survived.

In the early 1980's, a new principal was appointed. Ethan Mings was the closest to my first principal at A.Y. Jackson, Don Hazel. I felt free again to experiment with curriculum and began teaching entrepreneurship under the guise of consumer education. I began to innovate new ways of engaging learners in the learning process. While at A.Y. Jackson, I had a roomful of resources due to the high-powered roles played by parents. At Simcoe, I did not have this advantage, and I really didn't need it. Students wanted to be engaged and I could find ways to do that so that we would have highly interactive classes. Ethan Mings had restored the conditions and culture of open concept with some structure.

At Simcoe, I decided to take a small risk and guide my students in writing their own autobiography. I would then read it, review it and meet with them individually, to discuss what I considered to be the salient points. By entering into this dialogue, I was able to achieve two outcomes: First, to get a broader perspective of the person and to get a handle on their strengths and talents. The second unanticipated outcome was that I gained a great deal of trust and respect from my students, as reciprocation for my genuine interest in them.

Based on the above experiences, I was able to help students identify their distinct strengths and talents. They shared these strengths and talents with their peers and, in the process, complained very little when I placed them in diverse teams for various activities and simulations.

One of my successes at the secondary school level came from my experience with an Introduction to Business Grade 9 class at Governor Simcoe. Using the above model alongside a number of activity-based learning strategies, the class was able to create a community that would cater to the needs of their members. This community consisted of a mayor and his/her council, all types of businesses found in the community, and, of course, consumers who would become buyers of goods and services. Prior to the start of this semester-long community enterprise, participants could earn income by performing such activities as attending class, completing assignments on time, and successfully engaging in various classroom activities. They would use these accumulated rewards to save in the bank, prior to making necessary purchases during the game. Of course, those who volunteered to keep track of all this would also earn extra money. That alone saved this teacher's lack of organization from showing up. Little did I know at the time, that this activity, that the students called New Cali, would become the necessary activity for future teachers in all teachable subjects. The success of this New Cali initiative spread among students. The Introduction to Business program that began with one class that year grew to two the next year, and three, the following year.

My lifelong journey in the field of education has engaged my physical, emotional, professional and spiritual self. As an entrepreneur working inside a highly structured educational bureaucracy, I always sought to create new pathways for myself and for my students. It became a game for me to discover ways around existing rules and regulations that hampered learning in the classroom environment. These rules and regulations exist throughout the educational bureaucracy from the Ministry of Education on down. These decisions impact directly on the classroom as Beare and Slaughter (1993, p. 35) point out:

> In fact, the big school was designed and organized like a factory. Thus the terminology used in schools is based upon metaphors both from factories and medieval times. We should not expect the public school system to survive in its present form. Globally, most of these schools seem to have the same agenda: to set priorities, to trim expenditures and save scarce education dollars. To be good economic managers, those running educational enterprises have borrowed the devices of business, commerce and finance departments.

Within these conditions and cultures, teachers are expected to engage learners in the learning process. How can one be expected to create conditions and cultures that engage, enable and empower both teachers and learners when their environment is that of a factory and not a safe learning lab that nurtures and supports an enterprising learning environment?

Kenneth Sirotnik (2000) points out the difference between the industrial metaphor of the past and the knowledge-based metaphor of the 21st century. According to Sirotnik, society constantly reinvents itself by means of creativity and innovation, renewal and regeneration. The same cannot be said about our educational infrastructure. We only need to look at staff development methods. The RAND study reviewed factors associated with success and failure in staff development (McLaughlin and Marsh, 1978). The study identified five factors associated with effective staff development initiatives, including the teacher as expert (the inside-outside approach introduced by Hunt, 1987), and local adaptation, in that teachers and administrative staff worked together to adapt an innovation that is brought to the school, based on the local needs of the community. The study also proposes that professional learning is a long-term non-linear process that takes several years to achieve.

The need for staff development exists at every level of the school. It should include not only teachers but administration and support staff, working together in a collaborative fashion. Finally, the study points out that staff development never ends. Development is used as an integral part of the problem solving and improvement process within the school. The key criteria, identified by RAND, led to these five questions: Is the teacher acknowledged as a source of expertise? Do teachers have responsibility for local adaptation? Is their professional renewal long term? Is the purpose of professional renewal to promote teacher/administrator growth, rather than to correct defects? Is staff development visibly supported by the administration through their actions? These questions point to Hunt's (1987) approach of inside-outside, as opposed to the present outside-inside approach.

In the fall of 1987, I was invited to attend the opening of Ontario's Legislative Assembly as a guest of James Bradley, the incoming Environment Minister. Little did I know why I was invited until I heard the lieutenant governor read that Entrepreneurship Education would be a course at the secondary school level. Due to my excitement, I almost fell over the balcony after the announcement. I could now legitimately pursue what I had been already doing. I could develop a program for both adolescents and adults.

I decided to go to Brock University in order to meet with the Dean of Business to see if he could recommend someone in his faculty who could help me develop the program. To my delight, the business school had just hired Professor Kenneth E. Loucks, an entrepreneurial expert. After a few meetings with Ken, I decided to use the Adopt-a-School Program and adopt Brock University. A formal meeting was held at Governor Simcoe and, together with an advisory board of parents, we embarked on developing an entrepreneurship program for both adolescents and adults. All this would not have taken place without the moral and financial support of Ethan Mings. Ethan became my enabler as he convinced the bureaucracy to provide me with free reign to develop this innovative program.

During the period of 1976 to 1990, we were fortunate to have strong leadership at the Lincoln County Board of Education. Beginning with Roger Allen, Director of Education, and followed by his successor, Gary Holmes, there existed a supportive culture for teachers with innovative ideas in their classrooms. This made it easier for administrators to support their staff's creative expression.

Another major event unanticipated by me changed my future in the field of entrepreneurship education. I had been working closely with Dr. Loucks on a regular basis, when I heard the news that Brock had applied for provincial funding to become a Centre for Entrepreneurship. A special event was organized at the St. Catharines Club, where the Chancellor Robert Welch, Sr. and the university community invited local business people and entrepreneurs to get their moral support for this initiative. During the course of the presentation, one entrepreneur asked a key question: "What if you are not successful with your bid?" No one seemed to have an answer from the university and, suddenly, one of the entrepreneurs responded. "Forget government funding. Why don't we raise the money?" One of the first contributors was Henry Burgoyne, whose contribution of $500,000 led to the creation of the Burgoyne Centre for Entrepreneurship in 1988. This centre became a gateway for me to meet with leaders at the Faculty of Education at Brock.

It would be two years of work with Vic Cicci, Head of Continuing Education at Brock's Faculty of Education, that would lead to my development of an Additional Qualifications Course and, later, to a Specialist Program in Entrepreneurial Studies. Now, I had found another partner at the Faculty of Education to continue on my journey.

At Governor Simcoe, we had to bring more teachers into the Business Department where I had become its head. In addition, there was a lot of interest in the Adult Education Department and I began teaching half of my time in the Adult Education program.

In 1990, several members of the Burgoyne Board approached my Director of Education, Gary Holmes, with a proposition to second me to Brock University, where I would continue to develop the teacher education program in Entrepreneurial Studies and become an executive director of the 'New Enterprise Store', a partnership between Brock, The Lincoln Board of Education, Niagara Peninsula Industry and Education Council, and the Government of Canada.

I had looked at a number of diverse issues in our community, which was being ravaged by downsizing and high unemployment. If we could help these people find a direction in their lives in a safe environment, we might find a new source of business start-ups. In 1991, with 20 participants, we opened the New Enterprise Store on Niagara Street in St. Catharines. I saw the store as potentially a learning lab where we could not only help people become self-employed, small business owners or entrepreneurs, but we could analyze and synthesize our performance. The popularity of the New Enterprise Store went beyond the boundaries of Niagara, and at one time, we counted over a dozen locations across Canada.

In 1992, administrative changes in the Burgoyne Centre led to the Dean of Business becoming the acting director, leaving me to wonder what would happen to the work I had been doing? One day, the dean came to visit me and asked me if I wanted to remain and develop new courses in entrepreneurship for the Faculty of Business. He said that the new president wanted more of an internal focus, rather than a community one. I agreed to stay on and teach two distinct courses in entrepreneurship. All my other activities at the Faculty of Education and the New Enterprise Store would continue.

Around the same time, I planned meeting with our regional director of Human Resources Development Canada (HRDC), as it was called at that time, to share a vision I had. I was totally surprised when I met Jim Williams that he shared a similar vision – 'to inculcate the entrepreneurial spirit into every sector of society'.

It was my intention to create an Institute for Enterprise Education outside the walls of academe, independent of any capricious action, which would be able to work towards an entrepreneurial society. Jim did not hesitate. He asked how much money I would need and to send him a budget. He shared my beliefs and values, along with the vision and mission, and would fit it in within the rules of his bureaucracy.

In August of 1993, the Institute for Enterprise Education was born. The Dean of Business, William Richardson, saw this as a no-conflict situation, and provided the Institute with two new computers and a printer as the university's contribution. It was an opportunity for me to pursue entrepreneurship from a totally alternate perspective. Until this time, I had worked almost in a state of unconscious competence. I had created conditions that enabled learners to interact with one another in simulations and other experiential exercises, to have fun doing it, and, in the end, to reflect on their experience and teach one another about their discoveries. Everyone in the class not only became a learner, but also a teacher. I had taken the traditional curriculum and course of study on the one hand, and my need to create an alternate learning environment, on the other. This practice needed a theory especially now that I was looking to alternate educational programs in the community, as well as at the undergraduate level.

In entrepreneurship, I had found a way to bring these experiences together. Each person would begin with themselves and what they saw as their contribution (talent, knowledge and skills) and seek to find either an idea or opportunity that was consistent with their contribution, then go out and find the needed resources and then, start their business. The methods were very similar to the simulations that the adolescents had been working with. I needed to find a theory that would be a model for this. The new institute would help me find it. At the institute, I would conduct further research of existing entrepreneurs in order to hone in on their distinct modus operandi.

I began in 1994 with a study of the emerging Niagara Wine Industry. It also became a project for my students in the undergraduate entrepreneurship courses that I had introduced at Brock. A phone call from Donald Ziraldo, the father of this new cottage industry, reassured me that we were on the right course. Little did I know at that time, but upon the release of the study's findings, the president of Brock would begin a campaign to build the Cold Climate Viticulture and Oenology Institute, known as CCOVI. By creating an awareness of the entrepreneurial spirit in Niagara, I was able to provide a living model of how a new industry would become a world-class model of transformation.

There were a number of major findings in this study that were consistent with my teaching and learning strategies. But, more importantly, the wine industry study provided a framework for transformation. Four years later, I would use these findings to develop the Enterprise Education component in the alternate Bachelor of Education, Enterprise Education Program at Brock.

What did we learn from the wine industry study? First, we discovered that transformative change, as in the birth of a new industry, comes from the edges of existing structures. This means that it is extremely difficult for an existing organizational structure to reinvent itself from within. There is just too much invested in effort, money and time to dislodge what already exists. Thus, you need to begin with a new entity that does not have the baggage that prevents the birth and growth of a new concept. The existing wineries were just too locked in to their existing paradigms of doing business.

Second, we found that people create what has not been created before while discovering new sources of opportunity, by exploring in an enterprising, imaginative and interdependent manner. This second finding hit a strong note. Entrepreneurs, as agents of change, see themselves as being free to improvise as part of their interactions with the environment. It was this freedom that I helped create in my secondary school classes that enticed my students to boldly go forward in their trial and error efforts, to discover solutions to the challenges I proposed.

The third finding hit home for me. I discovered that taking risks in creating new ventures enabled people to take the kind of initiatives that helped them identify future visions, which engaged their individual capabilities and talents. This third finding enabled me to find support for the need to engage each person on a journey of discovering his/her distinct strengths, talents, motivation and creativity. I had now found a compelling body of action research to support my teaching strategies.

In the fall of 1996, I was approached by Anne Sutherland, Senior Vice-President of the Royal Bank, to design a course for business bankers. I called this program 'Understanding the Entrepreneur'. It consisted of a number of interactive units designed specifically to engage bankers in an exploratory process that included an interview with an entrepreneur, prior to attending the session. In addition, the bankers had to complete a self-assessment instrument, The Kolbe Conative Index, which would enable them to discover their striving instincts.

Over the next four years, I facilitated over 80 sessions across Canada, meeting with 1600 business bankers in the process. The Royal Bank's commitment to this program was rewarded with an increased share of the small business market. My reward was 1600 new profiles of entrepreneurs that helped me to synthesize these findings, in order to better understand the mind of the entrepreneur. This research led me to read further studies of entrepreneurs by academics in Canada, the United Kingdom and the United States, in order to seek consistency. My work in the field of entrepreneurial research is contained in three refereed journal articles.

In my second year of teaching entrepreneurship at Brock University's Business School, I was approached by the program chair with the suggestion that I make entrepreneurship a rigid academic discipline. My response was that after my original study of entrepreneurs, it would be very difficult to find a one size that fit all. In fact, we also needed to consider the opportunity, the external environment, the entrepreneurial mind and access to resources, as each was a separate variable in and of themselves. How could we possibly make entrepreneurship a rigid academic discipline within the realm of this complexity?

The need for a theory outside the field of entrepreneurship itself led me on many journeys across the academic terrain. Only after these many iterations, did I finally discover the theory of complexity. In fact, I went as far as visiting its home base at the Santa Fe Institute. Here I learned from scientists and Nobel Laureates the true meaning and place for complexity theory. I had found the theory of entrepreneurship outside the field itself.

WHY A NEED EXISTS FOR A NEW THEORY

A brief discussion of the scientific method for comparison purposes begins as an essential framework in preparation for the introduction of complexity theory. The science of the industrial age relied upon the scientific method in order to establish objective truth. This method of questioning viewed systems in isolation from one another and their environment. There were two factors that became critical in conducting research: One needed to separate the observer from what was being observed, and a need existed to reduce every physical element to its lowest common denominator and use the parts to predict future behaviour.

The Newtonian mechanistic and reductionist system became the basis of scientific thought. The key components of this system included determinism, linearity, predictability and simplicity. By embodying these principles, Fredrick Taylor (Kelly & Allison 1998) was able to create the Scientific Management Model that continues today to influence many individuals, leaders and organizations around the globe, as they attempt to adapt to the realities of globalization. Taylor argued that efficiency came from knowing exactly what you want people to do and then ensuring that they did it in the best and least expensive way. He believed that the practice of management would become a science that rested on clearly defined laws, rules and principles serving as the framework.

What we are now facing, however, is a major economic and social paradigm shift, where the exponential growth of information technologies and knowledge has created an ever-widening gap in human understanding of the impact and nature of this change.

Paradigms are fundamental beliefs about the world (Kuhn 1962). They provide the needed rules and regulations, establish boundaries and indicate the behaviours needed to succeed. Paradigms also suggest metaphors that are helpful in framing problems that lead to their ultimate solutions. However, on the flip side, paradigms can blind individuals to facts, data and challenges that are not consistent with their thinking. Conflict between exponents of different paradigms can also lead to irrational debate. This debate is currently taking place at all levels of the scientific, political, economic and social spectrums, as the traditional Newtonian mechanistic paradigm is being challenged by the emerging complexity theory and the entrepreneurial metaphor.

A study by the Washington Centre for Complexity and Public Policy (2003) on behalf of the U.S. Department of Education concludes that current conventional policy planning methods used by decision makers in business, education and government are both inappropriate and ineffective. The study's findings point to a rise in the integration of knowledge across disciplines. The interdisciplinary nature of complexity theory and its adoption of a system's view, means that questions that are too big for one discipline to answer are resolved by connecting knowledge across physical, biological and social boundaries.

COMPLEXITY THEORY: A CONVERGENT PARADIGM

Complexity theory is the study of complex adaptive systems that have the ability to process and integrate new information into their existing repertoire. Complexity theory is the bridge between chaos and order and a brief description of this theory follows.

Our world is a complex system and, like our body, consists of a series of organizational structures (economic, political, social), which interact with one another, nationally and internationally. A major tenet of complexity theory is the system itself. It consists of a set of units and elements so interconnected, that a change in one unit produces changes in other parts. As an example, our body is a system of interconnected parts. These body parts are useful only when they are part of the body, as a whole. The same holds true for individuals in society who recognize the need to work together in order to achieve a particular goal.

Complexity theory was developed by leading scientists from diverse fields of study. This science studies what it describes as 'complex adaptive systems', which include cells, embryos, brains, ecologies, economies, political and social systems. These complex adaptive systems consist of diverse parts that are organically related to one another. Complexity is also a central principle of evolution that effectively demonstrates how, through a process of differentiation and integration, humans can transcend their evolutionary path. It helps to explain how organisms with a more integrated physiology or behavioural repertoire, tend to gain a competitive advantage over others.

A complex adaptive system is generally defined as a system of independent agents that act in parallel to create new possibilities in their environment. Our immune system is defined as a complex adaptive system. So is an enterprise. Like all living systems, complex adaptive systems work best in cultures of diversity where each person seeks to achieve their distinct mission (differentiation) within a network of stakeholders (integration). What emerges from these interactions for the individual participant could become a new market hit or failure as experienced by millions of sellers on the web. It is only by means of determination, learning and persistence within this network, that order, in the form of acceptance of the individual's concept, product or service, emerges. Often, it is a journey of many iterations and destinations before the trophy is won.

In order to understand the workings of these complex adaptive systems, we need to understand their constituent parts and how they interact with one another. Let us begin with the components. Agents are known as decision-making units and include individuals that make up an ecosystem for an enterprise. Rules determine how agents make choices. Each individual agent has his/her own rules of behaviour. People are distinct beings based on their genes, culture and gender, and it is this diversity within specific networks that enables new possibilities to emerge. Emergent properties are the result of individual agents, interacting with one another, each following their own sets of behavioural rules, creating a whole that is greater than the sum of their individual interactions. By understanding how these agents interact with one another, we begin to internalize a process that leads us towards a higher order. This higher order is achieved by means of self-organization.

THE MEANING OF SELF-ORGANIZATION

Self-organization refers to how a system of agents organizes itself into a higher order. There are three distinct characteristics of such a system. Complex behaviours can result from individual units (agents). As a result, from a diversity of these individual inputs, interactions and interrelationships, a possible solution emerges. The robustness of the system, as a whole, is greater than the sum of its individual inputs.

The Internet is such an example. It integrates a wide breadth of knowledge, captures and displays a depth of information; processes information correctly, organizes information into a knowledge base and expands the reach across the globe. When you connect millions of people from around the globe, you enhance each individual's creative process by a power of thousands.

The critical variable that makes the system both complex and adaptive is the idea that agents (cells, ants, neurons, or individuals) in the system accumulate experience by interacting with other agents, and then change themselves to adapt to a changing environment. If a complex adaptive system is continuously adapting, it is impossible for any such system, including the education system, ever to reach a state of perfect equilibrium. The complexity view is that our external environments are not rational, are organic, not mechanistic, and are imperfectly inefficient.

Whether we look at economic, political or social systems, they are complex (a large number of individual units) and they are adaptive (individual units adapting their behaviours on the basis of interaction with other units, as well as with the systems, as a whole.) These systems have 'self-organizing properties' and, once organized, they generate emergent behaviours.

As a result of my study of complexity theory and its interdisciplinary nature, I crafted a relationship between this science and the emerging field of entrepreneurship. I was so excited that I created a new word: Entreplexity® – the joining of enterprise and complexity. I finally found a theory to explain the practice of entrepreneurship.

In 1994, we were successful in achieving a National Program in Youth Entrepreneurship. This enabled me to develop a special program for young people seeking to discover their niche in the world around them. Having gained a great deal of experience and insight from our New Enterprise Store model and my work with undergraduates at Brock, I crafted a model of entrepreneurial learning that began with extensive personal reflection sessions designed to enable the learner to discover their distinct strengths, talents, motivation and creativity, as a starting point. Once people had a sense of self, we provided them with an opportunity to explore the external environment in order to discover opportunities that matched their distinct capabilities. These exercises would lead to the engagement of the creative process that would lead to the development of a concept that would be tested for viability in the respective environment. The final step would be the creating of an action plan, which would undergo further testing.

Armed with this program, we began advertising in papers and by word of mouth. It did not take long to find 16 students for this 6-month program. In fact, almost half of the students came from my entrepreneurship classes at Brock. Upon graduation, they were still searching to find their niche.

My next challenge was to find the right facilitator to deliver this program. You can imagine my delight when my first choice accepted the position.

Larry Reikopf was a graduate of our Entrepreneurship Specialist's teacher education program at Brock. We were fortunate to second Larry from his school board. I knew our class would work out well with Larry at the helm and I was not disappointed. He was truly a Pied Piper.

One of the rewards of this program for our students included a $5000 dollar stipend upon successful presentation of a business plan. Every person who started the program was successful in getting this stipend. It was an excellent beginning for our graduates who, in most cases, leveraged this with the help of family and the Royal Bank.

Our first class was a success, leading to more programs. We had found a way to help people find their niche and turn it into a vocation in pursuit of their own enterprise. What did we learn from our experience? We discovered that young people had not been afforded an opportunity to search and discover their distinct strengths, talents and motivation. While they had achieved an excellent education in the cognitive sense, they did not have an opportunity to discover their passion and purpose in life. Our research of entrepreneurs began to show valuable clues as to the mind of the entrepreneur, and we were beginning to use some of our findings in the development of these entrepreneurial curricula.

Our early efforts included the use of several human assessment instruments that included the Kolbe Conative Index, which measures striving instincts, and the Hermann Brain Dominance Instrument, which assesses our cognitive and emotional brain. Both of these tools were based on the work of Dr. Paul McLean's Triune Brain Theory and the work of Dr. Roger Sperry's left and right hemispheres of the brain. Together, these instruments provided our learners with a starting point on the journey of self-discovery.

In the spring of 1996, I met with Dr. Terrence Boak, Dean of the Faculty of Education and Vic Cicci, Head of In-Service Teacher Education at Brock University in St. Catharines, Ontario. The purpose of the meeting was to create an alternative teacher education program. The work with our Youth Entrepreneurship Program indicated the need for each person to discover their distinct genius before embarking on their life's journey. The Profit 100 Study identified 'intrinsic motivation' as the key attitudinal component as had a number of other studies, particularly by Mihaly Csikszentmihalyi (1990). It was our belief that when we included this component with the three-part Entrepreneurship Specialist's Program, we could develop an Enterprise Education component that could be connected with the existing Bachelor of Education curriculum.

Over the next year, we began to meet on a regular basis in order to discuss the feasibility of such an undertaking. In spite of a number of unsuccessful meetings with both Ministry of Education officials and Brock's president, with the addition of Dr. Sybil Wilson to the team, we were able to develop a pilot for delivery in 1998. This coincided with the arrival of David Atkinson as President of Brock University and the move of Terrence Boak to the position of Academic Vice President. It appeared that the planets had finally aligned themselves in our favour.

VP Boak was able to get the right approvals from the Ministry of Education and members of Brock's faculty agreed to deliver a pilot program for the fall of

1999. The most interesting part of this initiative was that this program would be taught jointly by Brock's faculty and facilitators from the Institute for Enterprise Education. We met on a number of occasions to become familiar with the nature of the program, the people who would deliver the courses, and to discuss the difference between this program and the Intermediate/Senior Teacher Education Program currently being offered at Brock. In one case, I was asked by a Brock faculty member why this was not a business agenda on my part. It was at this point that I was able to convey the meaning of enterprise. I had crafted a definition that stated that it was 'the taking of initiative to achieve a self-determined goal that is part of a compelling vision that enables one to achieve their meaning in life, while sharing these achievements with others in the community'. This definition seemed to satisfy most, that enterprise, indeed, was not a business agenda.

We began our program in the fall of 1999. We shared space at the Institute for Enterprise Education and at Brock University. Our first group of learners consisted of eight students. We took them through a program that would become our signature program, once it was decided that it would become a permanent appurtence to the Faculty of Education's existing Intermediate/Senior Program.

Two people played a critical role during this pilot program: Vic Cicci, who became acting dean once Dean Boak was appointed Academic Vice President, and Sybil Wilson, who was, at that time, a faculty member at Brock and Chair of the Senate. It was their enterprising spirit that kept both the Institute side and their faculty members engaged in this experimental program.

Once the program was completed, we reflected upon its apparent strengths and weaknesses. In addition, Dr. Wilson was able to engage one of her graduate students, Deborah Mindorf, to conduct a review of the program. This intensive interview process led to the conclusion that, indeed, this program should be included as an adjunct to the existing program. In the fall of 2001, we would begin the Bachelor of Education, Enterprise Education Program at Brock's Hamilton campus.

Over the next six years, more than 120 teacher candidates would become graduates of this program. During this period, we had many opportunities to provide these learners with an opportunity to reflect upon their experiences and share with us ideas for change. By the end of the sixth year, we were able to conduct personal interviews as part of a research study approved by Brock's Ethics Committee. These findings will follow after a description of the program itself.

A SHARED UNDERSTANDING OF THE MEANING OF ENTREPRENEURSHIP

It would be misleading on my part to insert a full research rationale at this point for the Enterprise Education Program without explanation. The research that I would gather, once the program was underway, would support the practice for enterprise education that I was able to develop. Prior to the design and delivery of Enterprise Education, I could only depend on my experiences in designing and delivering entrepreneurship curricula for The New Enterprise Store Program, the undergraduate entrepreneurship program at Brock and the Executive Enterprise

Program and Youth Enterprise Program at the Institute for Enterprise Education. In addition, I had about 2200 entrepreneurial profiles at the time.

My review of literature applies to both the fields of entrepreneurship and enterprise education at this point. It builds a more focused approach prior to the introduction of the program itself.

ENTREPRENEURS AND ENTERPRISING PEOPLE

Entrepreneurs, as agents of change and disruption, demonstrate the principles of complex adaptive systems. Not only are they capable of adapting to their respective environments by identifying needs or opportunities, but they can also create novel solutions to meet these desires. At the beginning, their behaviours may demonstrate a tendency to be chaotic and disruptive to outsiders. Once the opportunity is exploited, however, most bystanders see the merits and seem to embrace it.

Two critical factors are influencing today's exponential growth of new enterprises. These include an increased need for entrepreneurial talent to deal with today's emerging global realities, and the individual's conscious awareness of the need to discover one's meaning in a world of rapidly increasing discontinuities.

For the foreseeable future, we will continue to see a growing need for entrepreneurs to develop structures, systems, processes and strategies that can deal with the emerging complexities. This has tremendous implications, not only for those seeking to begin and grow an enterprise, but also for large monolithic organizations stuck in their existing paradigms and unable to take advantage of today's global opportunities.

The Green Paper – Entrepreneurship in Europe from the Commission of the European Communities (2003) pointed out that entrepreneurship was first and foremost a mindset. "Entrepreneurship is about people, their choices and actions in starting, taking over or running a business, or their involvement in a firm's strategic decision making. It covers an individual's motivation and capacity, independently or within an organization, to identify an opportunity and to pursue it, in order to produce new value or economic success."

Successful growth of an enterprise is dependent upon an individual's ability to creatively exploit emerging opportunities, while constantly adapting and implementing new products and/or services. The overall success of any enterprise is not based on the completion of a successful business plan, but upon the interrelationships between the intrinsic motivation of the entrepreneurs and their teams, and the supportive extrinsic motivation in the community that enables entrepreneurs to effectively grow their enterprises.

A study by the Organization of Economic Co-operation and Development (1989) of entrepreneurial behaviour provides lessons as to how each individual in society can become 'enterprising' by connecting their distinct talents, meaning and motivation to create new opportunities and possibilities for themselves. In short, people would need to be creative, rather than passive; capable of self-initiated action, rather than dependent; they would need to know how to learn, rather than expect to be taught; and they would need to be enterprising in their outlook, not think and act like an employee or client. The organizations in which they worked, communities in which they lived, and societies to which they belonged, would, in turn, also need to possess all these qualities.

A journey into the mind of the entrepreneur reveals a number of insights that societies can incorporate into creating the needed conditions and cultures for enterprise. Mihaly Csikszentmihalyi (1990) proposes that extremely high levels of intrinsic motivation are marked by such strong interest and involvement in their work, and by such a perfect match of task difficulty with the skill level, that people experience a kind of psychological 'flow', a sense of merging with the activity they are doing.

Teresa Amabile (1997) concludes that intrinsic motivation is conducive to an individual's creativity. Entrepreneurs generate and implement novel ideas in order to establish new ventures. All these efforts transpire in the mind of the entrepreneur. Entrepreneurs initiate the creative process, and thereby demonstrate how every person pursuing their purpose can do the same.

The next question that should be asked is: How is the influence of the external environment represented in the entrepreneur's experience? As per Mitton (1989), "Entrepreneurs see ways to put resources and information together in new combinations. They not only see the system (environment) as it is, but as it might be. They have a knack for looking at the usual and seeing the unusual; at the ordinary and seeing the extraordinary." The key, according to Shaver (1991), is to concentrate on the person in his/her situational context. Situational variables can determine the degree of motivational synergy that people will experience. If external incentives and supports are presented in a manner that enhances the entrepreneur's vision, it is likely to support motivation and creativity. For instance, entrepreneurial creativity may be weakened by many stringent controls, and government programs, regulations and taxation.

In the spring of 1999, I had occasion to meet Bob Magee, Chairman and CEO of The Woodbridge Group, one of the top three automotive parts manufacturers in Canada. He was introduced to me by his head of marketing, Martin Mazza, a graduate of Brock University, who had heard my keynote address at the Automotive Parts Manufacturing Association Annual Conference in Hamilton. I soon discovered that Bob shared a passion for his people and to that end, engaged me to help each person in management discover their distinct strengths, talents, motivation and creativity.

During that time, I worked with Bob and his team to engage his managers around the world to become enterprising, in order to develop their work teams to become more creative at every work location in the company. Working with Woodbridge deepened my practice to include large organizations as enterprising entities. Unfortunately, I discovered that enterprise cannot be easily incorporated into traditional organizational structures that lack the entrepreneurial spirit within. Woodbridge began as a worker buyout of a Monsanto division by its employees, and they worked as an entrepreneurial team to get past many obstacles and roadblocks. The culture they developed was entrepreneurial in nature, to begin with.

Early in my activities with Woodbridge, I struck upon a metaphor to complement the entrepreneurial practice and complexity theory. The metaphor I chose to reflect the organization's infrastructure was the jamming jazz metaphor. As part of the entertainment one evening during my facilitation session, I engaged a jamming jazz band, the Bob Keppy Trio, to play with one difference.

Some time after dinner, when the group was having coffee, Bob Keppy stopped and asked the group if they wanted to hear how they played jazz. Everyone was all ears as Bob explained that each player needed to be aware of his abilities and competencies. There needed to exist a strong sense of trust and a constant awareness of each other's distinct contribution. Along with a diversity of talent, a need existed for constant communication and interaction throughout the group.

One had to demonstrate an ability to adapt and be flexible to emerging opportunities and possibilities as they played on. Each player had to demonstrate a strong sense of meaning and motivation. There needed to exist a compelling vision of where the trio wanted to end up. They may not be aware of how they would get there, but, like a beacon, it would be waiting for them to find the right combinations on their journey. What was clear to me was that every person was responsible for his/her direct contribution, and, together with the others on the team, they could form alliances to achieve their ultimate purpose. Improvisation became the name of the game, always keeping the final destination in mind. Leadership would change as the needs of the group changed. Every person in the group needed to be not only aware of their personal strengths, but also their limitations, and encourage those with complementary talents to take the lead when the need arose. And the final point was that, as leaders, we needed to have a great sense of humour to carry us through the toughest of challenges. Everyone ended the evening in a reflective mood. There were very few questions.

The next day, the participants were confronted with a three-hour, live production game. Of the four groups, only Bob Magee's group organized itself as a jamming jazz group. It was remarkable. Bob stepped aside and let his group self organize into the various roles. Bob chose the role of innovator for himself, while another participant, who had demonstrated strong management capabilities, took the lead. Needless to say, Bob's team blew away the competition. Upon reflection, the other groups finally saw the benefits of this model. In the end, I was convinced that the practice of entrepreneurship and the leadership strategies of the jamming jazz metaphor found support in complexity theory. A practice in search of a theory had arrived. By the summer of 1999, I had this part of my journey wrapped up. I could now focus my energies on the creation of curriculum for the Bachelor of Education, Enterprise Education Program that would begin that fall.

RATIONALE FOR TEACHING AND LEARNING ABOUT ENTERPRISE

Two empirical studies provided a foundation for teaching and learning about enterprise. In the United States, a five-year national longitudinal study of adolescents in grades 6, 8, 10, and 12, was conducted relating to how they form ideas about future schooling and work. The researchers, headed by Charles Bidwell, Mihaly Csikszentmihalyi, Lowry Hedges and Barbara Schneider, made the following recommendations which include the need to develop high school curricula that stress creativity, adaptability, learners' distinct intelligences and emotions. They also proposed the need to link disciplines in order to discover common threads among subject areas and to master synthesis, as well as analysis. This enabled young people to move from one career path to another. Self-directed learning and team-based projects, based on the diversity of the group, should be practiced in every subject area. School-to-work programs should be restructured in a manner that connects the students' distinct talents, in order to lead to challenging, enjoyable and satisfying experiences.

We must constantly provide learners with ongoing opportunities to discover what they enjoy doing for its own sake, not just getting good grades. Children, who are provided challenges, are more likely to seize new opportunities, seek new ways of doing things, work on tasks with unclear solutions and inspire others to work on different challenges. These are the activities of an emerging workplace. We need to encourage parents, teachers and counsellors to advise young people on how to use their time to seek out future job options. By discovering more play-like experiential learning activities, which leads to spontaneity and creativity, we help to build self-confidence and educational attachment on the part of the learner. By encouraging parents to play a greater role in the life of their children by learning about their interests, allows parents to nurture a supportive environment.

An essential goal in the transition from school to a productive adult life is to develop curiosity and interest not only in learning, but, in life, as a whole. This is no mean task, since currently schools often do the opposite - dampen curiosity and lead students towards cynicism and disinterest. The best antidote against disengaged boredom is a combination of hard work and playfulness. To the extent that teenagers can develop intrinsic motivation, through self-directed exploration of knowledge and through extracurricular activities, they will enjoy what they do for its own sake.

The second study entitled 'The Effects of Entrepreneurship Training and Venture Creation on Youth Entrepreneurial Attitudes and Academic Performance', conducted by Howard Rasheed (2001) of the University of South Florida, focused on whether entrepreneurship education contributes to the development of entrepreneurial characteristics among youth, and whether it contributes to improved student academic performance. The research addressed the following questions: Can entrepreneurial training affect the personality traits or attitudes commonly associated with becoming an entrepreneur? Can teacher and classroom variables influence these psychographic traits and does teacher training and experience matter?

The study sample consisted of 9 schools and 28 classes, ranging from grade 3 through 8, of the Newark, New Jersey public school system. Within this group of schools, entrepreneurship education and training had been implemented for 450 students as a strategy for improving the academic status of an underachieving school population. From this sample, a sub-segment of 147 students was randomly developed to test for the effects of entrepreneurship education on academic performance. Ninety-one (91) students were from the treatment group that participated in the training and fifty-six (56) were from a control group.

Their findings include the following: Students receiving entrepreneurial training have a significantly higher motivation to achieve; a significantly higher sense of personal control; and higher self-esteem. Students, along with teachers who have entrepreneurship training, were more innovative and had more personal control, and the effects of entrepreneurship classes on academic performance produced the following results: Reading improved by 16 percent, Language by 15 percent, Spelling by 15 percent, Mathematics by almost 19 percent, Social Studies by 19.5 percent and Science by 39 percent.

Allan Gibb's pioneering work in the field of Enterprise Education at the University of Durham, United Kingdom, demonstrated that enterprising behaviours, skills and attributes could be supported throughout the education curriculum from the primary level upwards. Thus, Enterprise Education could be introduced into the standard mathematics, history, geography, languages and other curriculum via pedagogical processes, which stimulate the cultural essences of the small firm, the holistic task structure of the entrepreneur and action-oriented learning modules. The axioms upon which these models were based have been the vocational training programs, with a focus on simulation, on how these 'skills' would be used in the external environment through self-employment.

While the Institute for Enterprise Education found precedents as to how 'enterprise' could successfully be integrated into the educational system, we faced a number of challenges. The first challenge was definitional in nature. A battle still rages as to the definition of entrepreneurship. Academics, as well as practitioners, continue to debate this definition, confusing the differences between small business ownership, self-employment and entrepreneurship. We decided to leave this definitional challenge for another time.

Based on our understanding of the entrepreneurial field of study, we relied on our review of the various fields of study to separate enterprise and entrepreneurship. We concluded that enterprise should be delivered across the curriculum in order that we nurture the growth of individuals for all fields of endeavour, while entrepreneurship should be taught as a discipline for those individuals seeking to create an enterprise.

The need for a definition of enterprise became apparent. From our collective experience in this field, the following became an operating definition of enterprise: Taking initiative to achieve a self-determined goal that is part of a future vision, in order to achieve one's own meaning in life, while sharing its outcomes with others in the community. During the Bachelor of Education, Enterprise Education Program, our graduates began to share their definition of enterprise.

The biggest challenge lay within the educational system itself. The system must embody the principles it seeks to teach. The challenge is that we are dealing with an organic discipline within the confines of a mechanistic, hierarchical and bureaucratic structure. The educational system attempts to impose a command and control approach towards an ecological process that is totally antithetical to it. It was this environment that posed the greatest obstacle in delivering the Enterprise Education Program.

THE BACHELOR OF EDUCATION, ENTERPRISE
EDUCATION PROGRAM

The Bachelor of Education, Enterprise Education Program was an alternative program in teacher education. It was a partnership between Brock University's Faculty of Education and the Institute for Enterprise Education.

The program completed six iterations. As a result of a number of reflective sessions, two major changes were made. Two of the three enterprise courses were offered at the beginning of the Bachelor of Education, Enterprise Education Program in order that each teacher candidate could devote sufficient time to reflect upon their distinct essence of being, prior to engaging in various education-related courses.

Individuals also had an opportunity to reflect upon alternative careers during the course of this teacher education program. Besides teaching at the intermediate/secondary level, teacher candidates could choose to start their own enterprise, work as facilitators in organizations or in their respective professional fields as educators, human capital professionals or trainers.

ENTERPRISE STUDIES CURRICULUM

The first part of the enterprise curricula focused on the five E's of learning. The first unit was Environment. We began by creating a context for the learner. The creation of a context began by enabling each teacher candidate to become conscious of the emergent global environment and its resultant impact on the community and individuals who inhabit it. Through a series of interactive activities, participants co-created the elements that made up this *environment* under the title 'Global Scan'. As part of this activity, we reflected upon the why, how, when and what of these significant events.

The second unit was Economy. Once the context was developed, teacher candidates reflected upon potential strategies for success in this environment. Through a process of self-directed learning, participants sought out literature and research to gain a more ecological understanding. Participants also discovered the nature of today's network economy and the resultant new rules of interaction, by means of experiential and highly interactive activities.

The third unit was about Entrepreneurs. The study of entrepreneurs began with each teacher candidate conducting a personal interview with an entrepreneur in their community. By gaining insights into the workings of an entrepreneurial mind, teacher candidates observed first-hand their intrinsic motivation, the entrepreneurial process and their interaction with the environment. It was this contextual approach that provided insights into the need to have a strong sense of self, prior to embarking on a journey into the unpredictable external environment.

The fourth unit dealt with Enterprising Behaviours. The environment, economy, and entrepreneur provided the underlying framework for the enterprise unit. The enterprise unit was the heart, mind and soul of the program. It was here that the teacher candidate become immersed in a comprehensive process of self-discovery by means of a series of validated assessment tools and reflections that dealt with one's thoughts, emotions, perceptions, and instincts (our four human faculties). The purpose of this extensive experiential process was to become conscious of their distinct essence of being; discover their individual needs, strengths, talents, and values; discover their meaning and purpose; define their mission; connect their distinct characteristics with others in a diverse team environment; and develop their own context for learning and teaching. Upon completion of this unit, each participant was able to develop a composite personal profile that began the first leg of their journey into enterprise. These experiences also became the foundation for assisting their own learners to begin the process of discovering their essence of being within the context of the classroom and the community.

The final unit dealt with Entreplexity®. The purpose of this unit was to unite all 5 'E's' around the underlying Complexity Theory and the practice of entrepreneurship. The metaphor of the jamming jazz band was used to describe the nature of an organic, humane organization that nurtured each person's talents, along with their distinct contribution to the musical repertoire created by the band.

In Collin's (2001) studies of over 1,400 Fortune 500 companies over a 30-year period, he concluded that no innovation of any kind is possible without a humane organization and continued innovation in the practice of management. This finding encapsulates the purpose of the first part of Enterprise Education.

ENTERPRISE EDUCATION AND TEACHING CURRICULUM

Enterprise Education and Teaching was the second part of the enterprise education curriculum. The purpose of this unit was to connect the learning of the previous course. It was in this program that teacher candidates were provided with interactive learning challenges that enabled them to pursue and engage their talents and mission around team-based activities. The results differed depending upon the composition of the group and their methods of engagement of interaction. Each group could achieve a higher order, but their journey was as distinct as the nature of the group and their interactions.

The key was to provide the group with an environment that nurtured their distinct creativity in order to achieve maximum effectiveness. Teacher candidates gained an inherent understanding of their environment by means of its interactive nature, where the teacher acted as a facilitator. Learning objectives were negotiated. The focus was on process and each participant was encouraged to generate knowledge. Learning was based on a need-to-know basis. The sessions were flexible with a strong emphasis on theory into practice. Mistakes were learned from and tolerated. These activities were translated into the creation of experiential projects to be used in the classroom. Teacher candidates also participated in community-based initiatives, in order to develop a context for learning using their community. It was in this unit that participants, working in teams, created their version 'New Cali', based on their teachable subjects.

JOURNEY INTO ENTERPRISE CURRICULUM

This part of the curriculum was delivered during the course of the school year. Participants were expected to spend a three-week internship in a field related to the participant's teachable subjects. This was a more in-depth opportunity to develop a context for the participant as to how they might create activities and a learning context for their students. The teacher candidates were required to develop a personal action plan or a business action plan, depending upon their choice of vocation upon completion of the Bachelor of Education, Enterprise Education Program.

KILLING THE GOOSE THAT LAID GOLDEN EGGS: CANCELLATION OF THE PROGRAM

In the spring of 2007, after conducting interviews with promising candidates for the 2007-2008 academic year, I was disappointed to learn that our Enterprise Education Program would be cancelled. The reason given by then Dean of Education, Dr. James Heap, was that after consultation with the registrar's office, we were not getting sufficient numbers to warrant this program. He had relied on previous figures that were quantitative in nature, rather than measuring the qualitative benefits of the program for our graduates.

This decision was made without any consideration that we had obtained strong commitments from 22 students that they would make Enterprise Education their first choice. If I had known of this decision by the dean, I would have asked each interviewee to make a deposit towards their full tuition. Needless to say, the other members of the Brock faculty were shocked. One member of Brock's contract teaching staff resigned. It was indeed a sad year for Enterprise Education. We had lost momentum to inculcate the spirit of enterprise into the educational sector of our society.

ENTERPRISE EDUCATION SURVEY AND RESULTS

In order to complete this almost 10-year experience with Enterprise Education, in partnership with Brock University, I undertook to conduct a study of our participants' perception of this program. This required me to complete the necessary application and submit it to the Ethics Committee at Brock University before conducting the study. After obtaining Ethics' approval, I proceeded to conduct a study of our participants after I submitted their final grades to the office. The findings of the study are synthesized below.

A questionnaire was designed using a four-point Likert-type scale. The four choices provided included strongly agree, agree, disagree and strongly disagree.

The questions were designed and partially based on a focus group session held with a previous year's class. The responses' clusters included the following categories: Learning About Me; Learning About Enterprise; The Enterprise Learning Community; Learning Through Enterprise; and So What? Now What? Who Cares?

The first response category, Learning About Me, included responses to the following matters: I gained a better understanding of myself; increased awareness of my interests, strengths and talents; developed more confidence in myself; and developed my distinct creative abilities. Seventy-seven percent strongly agreed and twenty-three percent agreed with the above statements.

The second response category, Learning About Enterprise, consisted of the following issues: Developed enthusiasm about Enterprise Education as a teaching strategy; deepened my interest in the subject matter of the Enterprise Education component of the teacher education program; developed leadership skills; and put more effort into the Enterprise Education component than the other courses. Fifty percent of the respondents strongly agreed with these statements, forty-five percent agreed and five percent disagreed.

The third response category dealt with the Enterprise Learning Community. The questions were related to development of new friendships; learning to value new viewpoints; classroom provided opportunities for positive interacting; and being stimulated to learn more about Enterprise Education. Seventy-five percent agreed with the above statements.

The fourth category, Learning Through Enterprise, included the following questions: Assignments were challenging and interesting; the amount of materials covered in the program were reasonable; the level of difficulty of the program was appropriate; became more interested in community-based projects involving enterprise; and learned more about the meaning of enterprise by means of enterprising activities. Forty-six percent of the participants strongly agreed, forty-six percent agreed and eight percent disagreed.

The So What? Now What? Who Cares? category consisted of the following questions: Overall this was an excellent program; I would recommend this program to incoming teacher candidates; and this program prepared me to deal more effectively with the existing classroom environment. Eighty-five percent of the participants strongly agreed with these statements, and fifteen percent simply agreed. Based on the findings above, while there is always a need for improvement, the facts speak for themselves. The vast majority of participants strongly agreed that this program made a difference in their personal and professional lives – a compelling argument why this Enterprise Education Program needed to continue, perhaps at another institution.

CONCLUSION

Reflecting on my journey into the field of Enterprise Education left me with mixed emotions. When I looked at the experiences that I encountered on this journey, I received a great deal of satisfaction. What I did not share in this story were the many trips I made to Europe to share the story of the Bachelor of Education, Enterprise Education Program. Perhaps the most remarkable event took place in Durham, England in the spring of 2002. Durham University was the home of Alan Gibb, the acknowledged father of Enterprise Education. After my presentation to a global group of academics, one Durham faculty member asked, "How is it that you can get a Bachelor of Education, Enterprise Education Program in your country and we, who started all of this, cannot?" At first, I was taken aback by this question until a thought crossed my mind. We were fortunate to have the right combination of people at Brock who shared a common vision and who worked towards its achievement, by convincing the higher order to change what appeared to be a non-negotiable stance into a negotiable stance. We simply had the right people in the right seats to make a difference. You might say the planets were properly aligned. We, ourselves, were enterprising by our practices. We could teach what we practiced and continue to learn.

The other source of satisfaction was our graduates, who, during their practicums and later, as professionals, continued to distinguish themselves in their field. The Institute for Enterprise Education partnered with one of our graduates, the Halton Board of Education and the Ministry of Education to bring enterprise into a Section 22 program in which the success of the program rested with the teacher and her team. For us, it was confirmation of how effective this program was with the at-risk component in schools, as much as with the existing regular classes.

But, I also concluded with a great deal of sadness. The program succumbed to the numbers game in spite of all our efforts. Vic Cicci, Marguerite Botting and Bob Mroz, on the part of Brock, worked very hard to make enterprise an integral part of this program. Their efforts led to a five-year approval of the program by the College of Teachers. Together, we embedded enterprise into the Ministry's requirements. In the end, all the great results and efforts were for naught.

A final comment. Over the span of the program, two of our graduates were recognized as the top teachers in the Intermediate/Secondary category of Brock University. I still remember one of the graduates saying: "If it wasn't for Enterprise Education, I would not be standing here today. I did not have the marks to get accepted into Brock's regular I/S program." How many other top teachers will be held back from becoming a part of our profession?

Editor's Postscript

As noted, this draft led to the last formal piece of Gene's writing completed as the major research project required in his graduate studies. He proudly accepted his Master of Education degree at Brock University's summer convocation of 2008, shortly before his death in October of that year. In the time that has passed since Gene's Enterprise Education program was cancelled, it seems ironic, but somehow predictable, that most, if not all elements of his ideas and curriculum plans have become incorporated into many offerings by the university. His principles and language (the words *entrepreneurship* and *enterprise* seem to have lost their tarnish) are now embedded not only in curricular approaches but in the language of administration regarding innovation, planning and priorities.

Gene was a visionary whose willingness to share ideas about learning and teaching was exploited in ways that separated who he was as a person and the ultimate value of his work. The program cancellation may have been brought about by a number of factors, including administrative whimsy and short-sightedness, brought on by the politics and pressures of higher education; simple co-opting of a very good idea; or most damning-a failure to understand, appreciate and learn from the very curriculum that was cancelled.

As the program wound down, Gene expressed a measure of indignation. He had gathered sufficient information and supportive data to "fight a better fight" for the life of the program and any rights associated with the work he had produced. His energies and other commitments to his own and other organizations, plus his own graduate studies program, were demanding and beginning to be compromised by the onset of poor health.

When Gene was completing his M.Ed. research, in spite of his good humour and attitude, it was evident that he was very ill. I nominated him for an honorary doctorate as faculty members are encouraged to do for exceptional individuals. I and others enumerated his long service to the community and university, as well as bringing attention to the precarious state of his health and the need to honour him while he was still around to experience the acknowledgment of his work. The nomination was not accepted. Following Gene's death, I reiterated my request and added that even a posthumous awarding of an honorary doctorate would bring recognition to his great contributions. I was informed that it was against policy to award such degrees posthumously.

My comments are a criticism of policymakers who fail to deal with questions about what it means to be well educated by well-intentioned and socially informed educators. Gene's case is too common and repeats the experience of great innovators who were not recognized in their own time. Gene's creativity, great independence and free thinking were perceived as threats by those who did not understand that for him payment was in the use of his work and the pleasure of witnessing the success of his ideas.

> *What we have done for ourselves alone dies with us; what we have done for others and the world remains and is immortal.*
> Albert Pike

REFERENCES

Amabile, T. (1997). Entrepreneurial creativity through motivational synergy. *Journal of Creative Behaviour Creative Education Foundation, 31*(1), 18–26.

Beare, H., & Slaughter, R. (1993). *Education for the Twenty-First Century.* New York: Routledge.

Cole, A. L., & Knowles, G. J. (2000). *Researching Teaching: Exploring Teacher Development through Reflexive Inquiry.* Toronto: Allyn & Bacon.

SECTION ONE

Collins, J. C. (2001). *Good to Great: Why Some Companies Make the Leap…and Others Don't.* New York: Harper Collins.

Commission of European Communities. (2003). *Entrepreneurship in Europe: Green Paper.* Brussels.

Csikszentmihalyi, M. (1990). *The Psychology of Optimal Experience.* New York: Harper and Row.

Csikszentmihalyi, M., & Schneider, B. (2000). *Becoming Adult: How Teenagers Prepare for the World of Work.* New York: Basic Books.

Delors, J. (1996). *The Four Pillars of Education. Learning the Treasures Within* (pp. 85–97). Paris: Report to UNESCO of the International Commission on Education for the Twenty-first Century.

Gardner, H. (1993). *Multiple Intelligences: The Theory in Practice.* New York: Basic Books.

Gibb, A. (2006). Entrepreneurship: Unique solutions for unique environments: Is it possible to achieve this with the existing paradigm? In *World Conference of the International Council for Small Business, Melbourne, Australia, June 18–21.* (keynote address)

Goleman, D. (1998). *Working with Emotional Intelligence.* New York: Bantam Books.

Greenleaf, R. (1977). *Servant Leadership.* Mahwah, NJ: Paulist Press.

Kuhn, T. (1962). *The Structure of Scientific Revolutions.* Chicago/London: University of Chicago Press.

Hart, T. (2001). Teaching for wisdom. *Encounter: Education for Meaning and Justice, 14*(2), 7.

Herrmann, N. (1988). *The Creative Brain.* Kingsport, Tennessee: Quebecor Printing.

Hunt, D. E. (1987). *Beginning with Ourselves: In Practice, Theory and Human Affairs.* Cambridge, MA: Brookline Books.

Kelly, G. A. (1969). *Clinical Psychology and Personality.* New York: Wiley.

Kelly, S., & Allison, M. A. (1998). *The Complexity Advantage.* New York: McGraw Hill.

Kolbe, K. (1993). *Pure Instinct.* New York: Random House.

Mitton, D. G. (1989). The compleat entrepreneur. *Entrepreneurship –Theory and Practice, 13*(3), 9–19.

OECD. (1989). *Towards an Enterprising Culture: A Challenge for Education and Training.* CERI Monograph, 4. Paris: Organization for Economic Co-operation and Development.

Porras, J., & Collins, J. (1994). *Built to Last: Successful of Visionary Companies.* New York: Harper Collins.

Rasheed, H. (2001). Developing entrepreneurial potential in youth: The effects of entrepreneurial education and new venture creation. *Proceedings of United States Association of Small Business and Entrepreneurship.* University of South Florida.

Sergiovanni, T. (1992). *Moral Leadership: Getting to the Heart of School Improvement.* San Francisco: Jossey Bass.

Shaver, K. (1991). Person, process, choice: The psychology on new venture creation. *Entrepreneurial Theory and Practice Journal Texas, 16*(2), 23-35.

Sirotnik, K. (2000). Making sense of education renewal. *Phi Delta Kappan, 80,* 606–610.

Toole, E. (2005). *A New Earth: Awakening to Your Life's Purpose.* London: Penguin Books.

IT ALL STARTED WITH A JOURNEY

OVERVIEW

The writing in this section was prepared by Gene as conceptual and practical scaffolding for the curriculum used in the Bachelor of Education, Enterprise Education Program as well as many other educational programs and presentations. Gene's grounding in, and appreciation of philosophy and the deep roots of enterprising ways of thinking and acting are in great evidence. The reader is led on a journey that is sometimes circuitous and that sometimes folds back on itself, as lengthy conversations with Gene often did. The reader will also notice Gene's liberal use of upper case, bold-face and italics for emphasis. He once claimed that he did this so readers would have an idea of what he wanted to emphasize. I asked him if those were cues to wave his arms around and make his conductor-like gestures. He made a note of my comment and said he would get back to me after his next spell of writing.

In the pages that follow, Gene lays out the many threads of thought that influenced and guided him. He weaves those threads into a coherent theoretical background illustrated by examples from real-world circumstances.

He begins by discussing *Possibilities* through considering *The New Network Economy*. He defines and elaborates the ideas of *Increasing Returns and Lock-In*, and *Information-based Technology* connecting them to *Creativity, Innovation, and Entrepreneurship*. He explores *Product Life Cycles, the Characteristics of the New Network Economy, Complexity Theory and Economics and Marketing Strategies* before moving on to his favourite focus: *People*.

The discussion of *People* begins with a section called *Transcending Evolution's Purpose* followed by *Understanding the Workings of Our Brain/Mind, Systems Thinking, Human Beings as Living Systems,* and wrapping up with a piece on *Ecosystems* and *Connecting Everyone and Everything in Today's Global Village*.

Using the catchwords of *Passion* and *Performance* he deals with *Developing Consciousness and Creativity* and *The Entrepreneurial Process* which he illustrates by using the *Enterprise Diamond*. His illustration sets up discussions that deal with *Stages of Business Growth, Motivation* and *Structuring an Entrepreneurial Organization*.

He brings his wide-ranging ideas home in sections that cover **Changing the Paradigm with Entreplexity® and How Complex Adaptive Systems Work** using his favourite metaphor of *The Jamming Jazz Band* which he called `` *A Metaphor for Creating Organizations with a Consciousness*.``

THE MYTH OF PLEIADES – ASTEROPE'S JOURNEY

There is a myth that has been passed through the ages to explain the cluster of stars known as Pleiades; a cluster of seven points of light in the night sky, of which only six can been seen with the naked eye. This version is about Asterope, daughter of the gods, who went against convention to make her own mark in the skies of history.

For many years, the gods Atlas and Pleione were happy; they were in love and healthy; they were worshipped and honoured by mortals, while managing to keep out of the game of politics and social climbing in which the other gods of their generation seemed to find themselves. Life on Mount Olympia was pretty good. Over the years, their family expanded with children, until there were seven little sets of pattering feet and giggling voices clambering around their home. These seven girls while bringing even more wonder to their lives brought much more exasperation for Atlas. The children grew up happy and content amidst the chaos of home, sure of their futures and their place in the world.

Then things started to change around Olympia. The mortals, who had begun travelling further and experiencing other ways of life, were changing their ways, wanting more variety and becoming discontent with the rigid rule of their gods. The gods began fighting amongst themselves, and the growing uncertainty was throwing everything off balance. Atlas left the peace of his own busy household and went to the other gods to try to find a solution. As his wife and children watched, they saw him change from a creative and passionate man to someone busy patching holes in the political, social, and economic systems to avoid a seemingly inevitable crash - in essence, he held the world on his shoulders.

His daughters were now grown enough to move into the working world. Alcyone became a lawyer, Electra an actor, Celaeno a saleswoman, Maia had six children of her own to care for, Merope became a bee keeper, and Taygete a dancer (later to become founder and first Mayor of Sparta). But, Asterope refused to choose a profession. Her father's pet, she suffered in silence as she watched him deteriorate under the pressures of holding past ways together; ways which would surely tear the fabric of their existence if they were to change. She had several short-term jobs. In some she liked the money, but hated the authority figures; in others, she loved the challenges of a new project, but hated that her ideas were never acknowledged. After Atlas had his first heart attack (which the family kept quiet for fear of frightening his mortal worshipers), he called his favourite daughter in to talk to her. "You are my brightest star," he said, "but if you stay here you will dim with the rest of us. Go out into the far reaches of infinity and find your passion. Only then will you know how to be happy amongst this growing chaos".

So began Asterope's journey. Her travels brought her much needed perspective about the way the world worked; how it was changing because of advances in technology and the new desires of the mortals. She saw that no longer were products the primary source of capital to these individuals, but that creativity and the power of the mind were worth so much more than any other invention.

In this changing landscape, Asterope saw that possibilities abounded. There seemed to be no end to the options she could choose for herself, in jobs and in other decisions. With every new person she met, new ideas formed and new opportunities opened.

This immersion in the lives of mortals led her to look at the world differently. Instead of thinking only about what was out there, she began to think about what she was made of intrinsically, how she and others had evolved to be the people they were and how her conscious mind really worked. She realized that she was unique in many ways, and that she cherished her uniqueness. She also needed to be integrated into other networks so that her uniqueness could find practical purpose in society.

Through her realization that she controlled her own future and that she could express her own creativity in whatever she chose to do, she found her passion in life. Although her exploration started by leaving the sanctuary of her home and visiting faraway places to see how others lived, in the end she was left to look even more deeply inward than out. She found her innermost passions and desires and her own purpose.

Asterope had been gone from Olympia for many years. She yearned to return, yet was afraid that she would not be able to change the other gods and their ways of old. She missed her parents and her sisters, but knew that she could no longer compromise her own purpose to live in their world. So, she returned home with reservations, but also with a strong sense of self and purpose.

This purpose was to learn about where her skills and passions could best fit into the existing society in Olympia, or how she could find her own niche on the edge of that structure.

As she discussed this philosophy with others in Olympia, she found that although many preferred to remain in their current situations, and some even resented her need for change, others joined in her endeavour to create something new for themselves. Her performance in this new system was a combination of her creativity, innovation and strategies of entrepreneurship, through which she began to develop her own path through the world, amid the chaos and uncertainty. She accepted that these obstacles could also be seeds of change that would grow into new directions for her and others to travel.

Asterope's progress led to changing the paradigms of government and business in Olympia, a new example by which others could base their search and self-discovery process and find their passion and destiny. When you look at the night sky, legend has it you will easily see Atlas and Pleione and six of their seven daughters, but Asterope is too faint to see. Her light is shining the other way, at the endless expanse of possibilities waiting to be discovered.

POSSIBILITIES: THE NEW NETWORK ECONOMY

All I ever learned about the New Economics,
I learned from Wired Magazine

Paul Samuelson's 'Economics' text is back, albeit as a collector's item. Those of us who were subjected to Economics 101 made Samuelson a millionaire. Scarcity was the operating term in his work, where physical things made up capital. Along with other traditional economists, he talked endlessly about the stability of the marketplace, the balance of supply and demand, decreasing returns, static equilibrium, perfect rationality and countless other observations which were dressed up with a lot of formalism. ***The real world no longer operates that way!***

Although there are a number of ground states or equilibria within the economy due to a natural mixture of positive and negative feedback, the economy, as a whole, can never reach an equilibrium as traditional economists would have us believe. In the words of Mitchell Waldrop, "Like it or not, the marketplace isn't stable .... the world isn't stable .... it's full of evolution, upheaval, and surprise." 1

Today's New Network Economy works differently, according to Paul M. Rohmer, Professor of Economics at Stanford and University of California at Berkeley. In the new economy, monopolies belong to those first in the marketplace. Writing a complicated piece of software or discovering specific gene sequences requires large up-front costs. After the initial work is done, the cost of each additional unit begins to decrease. To make the first copy of Windows, Microsoft invested hundreds of millions of dollars in research and development, testing, etc. Once Microsoft got it right, it could produce additional copies of Windows for pennies. These monopolies, like Microsoft, continue to grow for a period of time until they are upstaged by newer and much more effective monopolies.

Thus, as returns diminish in the physical economy based on materials and resources, they increase in a knowledge-based economy. The key distinction between business in the industrial economy and the knowledge economy is this: In the industrial economy, the price of resources was the determinant and monopolies were held in check. In the knowledge economy, possession of ideas and their rapid distribution into the marketplace gives monopoly power to the first pioneer in the field. Knowledge has replaced resources as the new source of capital. In this kind of emerging environment, success is based on increasing the knowledge capability of the product or service to the largest possible user base, thus monopolizing the demand.

..."The more we discover new things, the better we become at the process of discovery itself. Knowledge builds on itself. As a result, the capacity to create wealth and value increases over time - surely another reason for optimism,"[2]

Along with such foreboding terms as the law of 'diminishing returns' and 'diminishing marginal utility', economics gained the reputation as a 'dismal science' - and deservedly so. Its basis also came from Newton's mechanistic world view that separated human beings from one another and the universe itself. It gave credence to Darwinian Theory, which provided the pattern for dealing with scarcity: *fight until only the fittest survive*. It is this kind of reductionist thinking that continues to haunt not only the economists of today, but business, government and society throughout the developed world. Because we 'locked-in' to this paradigm, it will likely take decades to dislodge it. We are still playing by the rules of hunter gatherers.

Throughout history, a force has existed that couldn't be measured by the scientific discoveries of their day. This powerful force was responsible for creating innovations that constantly transformed stable societies into new entities, capable of expanding beyond existing boundaries. Whether they were explorers like Christopher Columbus, John Cabot, or Ponce de Leon, these emerging entrepreneurs continued to expand their own horizons and those of their financiers and leaders. As new frontiers emerged, threats of war continued to enforce these emerging boundaries and power structures of the day.

In the Industrial Age, standardization and mass production were the structure and system that responded to the needs of the markets. While Henry Ford was the inventor of production standardization, Newton's Mechanistic Model became the scientific materialistic basis for industry's existence. The system was simple: **Standardize the product, break it up into component parts, create specialized operations to make these components, and then go for volume.** This became the process by which Ford and others began to churn out hundreds of automobiles, taking this system to new heights.

By standardizing the shop floor, Ford also standardized all management decision-making functions. This approach meant that everything could be handled by standard procedures, and management attention would only be required when unanticipated discrepancies or events took place. To avoid repetition of these situations in the future, manuals were written dealing with such things as standards for product development, manufacturing, accounting, and all other processes and procedures.

This system worked extremely well in periods of economic stability. The odd downturn was followed by another upturn as the business cycle advanced. In cases where the organization was in the early stages of growth, innovations that led to product differentiation and value-added production continued to impact positively on the bottom line.

However, when competition appeared on the horizon, business leaders discovered they were in a commodity business, which led them on a trail of price reduction and cost cutting, leading to downsizing, while seeking sales outside these saturated markets. To add fuel to the fire, the North American automobile manufacturers and their suppliers began to face foreign competition from Europe and Japan. These new challenges were just the tip of the proverbial iceberg as described by Gerald Ross and Michael Kay:

> Rising fragmentation of the market, kicked off by a competitive search for the volumes to sustain the economies of scale at the root of mass production, had been

fed by a technical ability to produce variety. Variety begat the demand for more variety. This, in turn, stimulated greater technical innovation until the techniques of mass customization coalesced everything into a new approach to production."[3]

These changes in the marketplace underscored the need for both structural and systemic change in order to meet the needs of individual consumers, by providing them with an infinite range of possibilities. The current economic model, which most people still follow, fails to explain these emerging realities based on the traditional principles of economics. Today, we need to unlearn the lessons of the past and relearn principles of the new economics. We need to become more acquainted with the expanding pie principle and the law of increasing returns, as well as the laws of quantum physics and evolutional biology. Today's New Economy is driven by a whole set of engines that see the universe not as a mechanistic, reductionist system, but as a 'connected whole' where everyone, everywhere, is connected to everyone and everything.

Today's emerging entrepreneurs are no longer dealing with the scarcity of land, labour and capital. Today, they are turning knowledge into value added products and services. As Toffler pointed out in *The Third Wave*, we have moved from the age of muscle and money to the age of the Mind. **The mind, as a creative force, is capable of imagining new possibilities in a manner that creates value without the use of any physical ingredients.** Consider software programs and operating systems similar to MS DOS and Windows, which made Bill Gates the richest person in the world in the shortest period of business history. Bill Gates and thousands upon thousands of information age entrepreneurs literally created wealth from their thoughts.

More and more people are beginning to recognize the tremendous power that exists within us. **Our human mind is incredibly powerful and complex.**

We are beginning to unfold a universe based on what David Bohm and Karl Pribram call 'morphogenic fields' of energy that facilitate this connectivity. We no longer live by the rules where only the fittest survive; *we shape our future by the energy of our thoughts.* We not only become what we think about, but in the words of management guru Peter Drucker, we predict our future by creating it.

At the Santa Fe Institute (SFI), economists began to view the real economy, not as a machine, but as a kind of living system with all the spontaneity and complexity that can be found in the world of molecular biology. To SFI economists, "the economy is like the biosphere: always evolving, always changing, always exploring new territory."[4]

Those seeking to find academic courses related to the emerging new economics may be shocked to learn that one of the best sources of information in this field is ' *Wired Magazine*'. For the serious student seeking to immerse themselves in the rigorous detail of the subject, the Santa Fe Institute is the place to be. Brian Arthur, John Holland and other resident experts are well underway to rewriting the economics textbook for the twenty-first century.

INCREASING RETURNS AND LOCK-IN

The term *'increasing returns'* refers to the phenomenon of a product or service increasing in popularity simply because it is the dominant player in its market. **When a new technology or product opens niches for other goods and services, the people who fill those niches have every incentive to help that technology or product prosper and grow.** This principle of increasing returns, which was almost completely ignored by traditional economists, might help to explain the liveliness, the complexity and the richness in the real-world economy. It can be demonstrated by how well entrepreneurs stretch their business concept to include suppliers, distributors, customers, employees and financiers. **By showing these individuals the benefits of participation in your concept, you ensure their involvement and they, in turn, will promote your idea to potential users.**

There are many real-world examples of increasing returns, such as the development of the QWERTY keyboard; the VHS vs. BETA battle; the numerous high-tech companies in the Silicon Valley of California and Waterloo, Ontario, Canada; the gasoline-powered vs. the steam-powered engine battle; the IBM and Macintosh dominance in personal computers; and numerous other products and services. **Indeed, increasing returns make the majority of high-tech markets unstable, lucrative and easy to corner.**

Bill Gates and his team have used these economic laws to position Microsoft as the pre-eminent software program through Windows links. It is anyone's guess as to how long it will take before a paradigm-busting innovation will topple Gates from the industry's summit. It may be a small enterprise in Europe that has just developed a system to link all existing hardware and software applications, or it may be a user-friendly software program from Sweden that may change the way we interact with our computers.

The concept of *lock-in* is very much related to the phenomenon of increasing returns. *Lock-in refers to the fact that as more niches spring up and become dependent on a given technology, it becomes much harder to change that technology until something very much better comes along.* Just think how long the internal combustion engine has lasted!

INFORMATION-BASED TECHNOLOGY

The value of the network as a transfer agent of information is in its ability to link members around the globe, and, in turn, provide greater value to the hardware and software applications of existing users. For example, the value of a fax machine increases with every new purchase of a fax machine by a new user. It allows everyone to access more potential partners or customers. The Internet is another example. Every time someone else gets on the web, the potential exists for a larger marketing or networking opportunity.

The power of the network is described by Kevin Kelly, publisher of Wired Magazine:

As networks have permeated our world, the economy has come to resemble an ecology of organisms, interlinked and co-evolving, constantly in flux, deeply tangled, ever expanding at its edges. As we know from recent ecological studies, no balance exists in nature, rather as evolution proceeds, there is perpetual disruption as new species displace old, as natural biomes shift in their makeup, and as organisms and environments transform each other.[5]

This living systems approach taken by Kelly and others falls outside the classical views of economics that powered the Industrial Era. The network dynamic will continue to weave its way into the fabric of business and economics on a global scale. The old economics will slowly dissipate as the network powered by innovation displaces it. Nicholas Negropronti of MIT has pointed out that this natural move from 'atoms' to 'bits' would be a $1 trillion industry by the year 2000! Imagine making all of your life decisions on the Internet, comparing prices and features from across the globe.

There are a number of major successes out there in cyberspace already. Amazon.com is an example of how an entrepreneur with very little start-up capital, a database and a network can create a multi-billion dollar enterprise, worth more than the venerable New York Times that has existed for 150 years. Other examples of these monumental miracles, which our minds perform daily, are the turning of sand into silicon chips or thoughts into software applications. It is the network that determines who survives and who retrenches to try again another day.

CREATIVITY, INNOVATION, AND ENTREPRENEURSHIP

Even with all of the existing knowledge in the world, which is available to everyone, it is not sufficient to succeed any longer. There is a need to break out of our existing mental models in order to create new possibilities. Of course, this is much easier said than done. Most people lack the necessary will to do this, even though they possess the necessary knowledge and intelligence. This challenge will be addressed in more detail in the following sections.

There are many cases where failure to create and innovate has led to the demise of organizations. Over the past 50 years, less than 17 percent of the original Fortune 500 companies have been left intact. During the last decade and a half, almost 50 percent have been deleted from the list. Even in the case of Canada's fastest-growing companies (Profit 100 survey), more than 50 percent fail to make the list the next year.

Thanks to the turbulent global environment, the discontinuous and rapidly changing marketplace, and the networks themselves, the rules continue to change as individuals and environments continue to react and interact. As

Michael Porter pointed out in his study of global competitiveness, the need for innovation, identification of niches, and distinctiveness of products and/or services is critical to the continuing growth and success of the enterprise.

PRODUCT LIFE CYCLES

The rules of doing business have changed. The emerging game plan is the result of shrinking product and service life cycles. The following model demonstrates the needed cyclical process to maintain business viability:

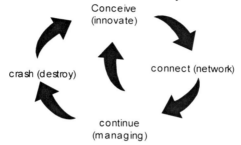

This highly interactive process was designed at the Institute for Enterprise Education to provide individuals and organizations with an opportunity to take advantage of the emerging networked economic paradigm. It is a powerful model used by successful entrepreneurs who recognize the uncertainty and unpredictability of the marketplace. The **conception** stage occurs when there is convergence between the person, an idea and an opportunity in order to identify a potential niche. In Asterope's story, this occurred when she decided to take her newfound ideas back to Olympia and turn them into concepts. The **connection** stage deals with the people, markets and resources needed to successfully exploit a niche, a situation Asterope would have had to deal with back in Olympia. The **continuing** phase focuses on managing the process effectively so that the customer gets more than they anticipated. This involves developing systems, processes, strategies, and structures that will provide a high quality experience every time. The **crash** stage can be likened to what Schumpeter describes as the process of **creative destruction,** i.e. going back to the drawing board to create the next innovation. The entire sequence begins all over again![6] Although not included in the Myth of Pleiades, Asterope and others on Olympia will have to continually destroy and recreate their systems and products in order to stay apace with their changing environment.

CHARACTERISTICS OF THE NEW NETWORK ECONOMY

1. It exists because of increased levels of innovation that are taking place on the edge of chaos and order in the economies of the world.
2. Traditional boundaries are blurred by emerging digitization and information technologies. This allows for rapid communication, transfer of funds, and deliveries of software and other services without governmental control and regulation (software sales across boundaries).

3. Interdependence is the critical force in establishing networks globally to ensure the successful penetration of niche markets. Networks of individuals, teams and organizations form to capitalize on emerging opportunities. For example, a product might be designed in the United States, while parts are sourced in Asia and final assembly takes place in Mexico. In each case, special relationships are forged to ensure the product's effectiveness.

4. We live in a world based on an expanding pie, not a fixed one. In the past, economists and business people viewed the market as a fixed pie where competition determined who got how much. The Darwinian paradigm held - the fittest survived. Today, the expanding pie has changed economics from what was a dismal science into an exciting science.

5. Two critical concepts associated with the new network economics are *the laws of 'increasing returns'* and *'lock-in'*.

6. Information-based technologies advance knowledge exponentially, thanks to a digitized network that facilitates participant interaction.

7. Creativity, innovation and entrepreneurship convert knowledge into new products, processes and services.

8. Shortened product life cycles. In many cases, a 6-18 month product life cycle is all you have. Once you have successfully exploited a niche, you need to consistently innovate again and again in order to create new possibilities for the next emerging niche. This involves undertaking a totally different modus operandi for your enterprise.

The differences between the old view of economics and the evolutionary approach to economics are illustrated by the above list of comparisons, which was compiled by economist Brian Arthur of the Santa Fe Institute. Understanding these differences clarifies the need to change our old paradigms of economics, which no longer help explain today's emerging realities.

This 'new economics' scares traditional economists because it will not allow them to predict anything. They are afraid that the inability to make precise predictions will then bring economics out of the realm of 'science'. What they do not understand, however, is that prediction is not the essence of science. **The essence of science is in comprehension and explanation, laying bare the fundamental mechanisms of nature.**

Explanation is what biologists, geologists, and astronomers do in their fields. The future of economics lies in explanations rather than prediction, and explanations can only be revealed by an awareness of past and present economic patterns and processes. Formal mathematics will have very little to do with it. A good example of this is the inability of traditional economists at the Department of Commerce in the United States to predict monthly labour statistics, due to the constant birth and demise of small enterprises.

OLD ECONOMICS	NEW ECONOMICS
Decreasing returns	Much use of increasing returns
Based on 19th century physics (equilibrium, stability, deterministic dynamics)	Based on biology (structure, pattern, self-organization, life cycle)
People identical	Focus on individual life: people separate and different
If only there were no externalities and all had equal abilities, we'd reach nirvana	Externalities and differences become driving force. No Nirvana. System. Constantly unfolding
Elements are quantities and prices	Elements are patterns and possibilities
No real dynamics in the sense that everything is at equilibrium	Economy is constantly on the edge of time. It rushes forward, structures constantly coalescing, decaying, changing
Sees subject as structurally sound	Sees subject as inherently complex
Economics as soft physics	Economics as high-complexity science

Adapted from M. Mitchell Waldorp, "Complexity, the emerging science at the edge of order and chaos", (Simon & Schuster, New York, 1992), p. 37

Organizations, today, face challenges of rapidly changing markets, global competitiveness, digitization and discontinuities, as a result of emerging technologies that close existing opportunities while exploiting new niches. Multinational giant Sony creates over 5000 new products each year, of which only about a dozen show profitability. Hewlett Packard, on the other hand, derives more than sixty percent of their annual sales from products created in the same year. To become successful today, these global organizations know that they not only need to be close to their customers, they need to work hand in hand with their customer. This partnership allows HP to design products based on problems and challenges faced by their customers in the workplace. Together, they discover the need and fill it. Then it's on to the next challenge. Meanwhile, other businesses in the same industry group become customers for these newly developed innovations.

In 'The Ten Rules of the New Economy', Kevin Kelly presents an outline of the new rules that include the following:

1. As power flows away from the centre, the competitive advantage will go to those who learn how to create on the edge.
2. As connections between people grow, the consequences of these connections multiply even quicker.
3. We live in a world of plenty. We can make copies of products with ever decreasing costs.
4. It pays to be generous and give things away.
5. Feed the network first to ensure its survival.
6. As innovation gathers momentum, abandon what is successful (crash & burn).
7. Place is replaced by space. The opportunities to meet anytime, anywhere leads to increased expansion of niches.
8. Innovation is the antidote to instability and change.
9. The most powerful technologies of the future are those that amplify, expand and extend relationships of all types.
10. Opportunities come before efficiencies. Discovery and creation of new opportunities rules the day.

What are the Strategies?

1. Complexity Theory and Economics
2. Marketing Strategies

Where we have the workings of the law of increasing returns, competition becomes a race to be first in the minds of the customer. 'To the victor go the spoils' is a term that gathers meaning for the firm that captures the greatest share of the market as quickly as possible, even if it does so with a product that is inferior or incomplete. Take a look at Netscape as an example. It gives away its browser and vaults to supply the greatest share of the market. Today, its merger with AOL makes it the product of choice for browsers and service software that it sells. These kinds of interactions are driving the falling costs and increasing returns as more and more people log in. Microsoft is facing a number of legal hurdles as governments prevent it from controlling the Information Highway. Microsoft is a monopolist where operating systems are concerned. Other firms can enter the market and can compete by selling products superior to Microsoft, but they have as much a chance of breaking Windows as one has of changing the letters around on the QWERTY keyboard.

On the other side of the ledger, the legal battle the government waged with Microsoft was for far greater territory than the Internet. Microsoft was a late entrant in the Internet game and sought to persuade us that its browser should be part of a Windows package, locking in the users of this monopolistic product.

As Rohmer points out, this is what economists call 'monopolistic competition'. It is what Sun Microsystems, Netscape and AOL, and Oracle are attempting to do to leverage the emerging power of the net. The key to their successful exploitation of niches is that the cost of replication is low.

Thus, the major point of competition in the New Network Economy is at the product introduction stage.

In the industrial economy, the market price determined how much of a product people would buy and how much companies were willing to make. The role of government was to control monopolists and ensure that the price would be freely determined. **There is no such equilibrium price in the knowledge economy.** Thus, we need alternative ways to reward innovation and tolerate existence of monopolists. In this kind of environment, we have what Schumpeter called 'creative destruction'. **We replace existing monopolists by new monopolists selling products and services that meet and, at times, exceed the expectations and needs of our customers.** Ideas and innovation help to create and generate new possibilities that are a response to the expectations and needs of customers. To join this game and become successful, we need to internalize a culture of innovation within our own organizations.

There is still a need for both financial systems and regulations. The financial system needs to provide the angels that help small enterprise to emerge and grow. It needs to raise capital. It needs to tolerate failure. Government needs to nurture and grow an environment that encourages this growth, tolerating failures, rewarding risks, and keeping taxes to a minimum at this incubation stage. Their payback will come three to five years from now, when they will be rewarded with taxes from these larger small enterprises and their employees.

In this world of emerging niches, exploitation of one new niche leads to the emergence of many others. Soon new players emerge to create new products and services. The only question becomes, "How many niches will open up?" This fragmentation of the marketplace ensures that new kinds of structures emerge within existing organizations to take advantage of these opportunities. **Today, the emerging structures need to be entrepreneurially driven and molecular in nature, a concept that will be explained in later sections.**

THE TWELVE THEMES OF THE NEW ECONOMY

The twelve themes discussed below are based on Donald Tapscott's, "The Digital Economy".

THEME 1: Today's New Economy is Knowledge-Based

This includes such things as smart cards (debit cards), smart houses (monitors), smart cars (electronic sensors), smart tires (air pressure changes based on the nature of roads), smart phones (digital communications), smart pucks (contain chips that send back information to certain computers), smart whistles (centre computer identifies referee during a football game).

THEME 2: Digitization

Digitization is responsible for the move from atoms (physical) to bits (information). Bits are beginning to carry more and more information, including graphs and photographs.

Old economy information was analogue-based (atoms). People communicated by moving their physical presence into rooms, speaking over analogue phones, sending letters, exchanging cash and cheques, and listening to and playing 45 rpm records on mechanical record players.

In the new economy, information is in digital forms (bits). When information becomes digitized, vast amounts of information can be squeezed or compressed and transmitted at the speed of light. This process allows for creation of multimedia documents. Information can be stored and retrieved instantly, providing access to information from around the world. Examples include email and the Internet.

THEME 3: Virtualization

1. Virtual data entry workers - anywhere around the world.
2. Virtual bulletin board – hyperlinks.
3. Virtual corporation - the grouping of several enterprises on the Internet in order to create an integrated business.
4. Virtual government agencies - Industry Canada's Strategies offers information services from governments, agencies and businesses.
5. Virtual Markets - located in cyberspace.
6. Virtual Reality - Meet in real time at your own place with others from around the globe.

THEME 4: Molecularization

The new economy is molecular in nature. The old corporation is breaking up or disappearing. Few are getting larger. They are being replaced by dynamic molecules and clusters of individuals and entities in order to form the basis of economic activity. The organization can fund these entrepreneurial units on the edge and watch them identify opportunities and exploit niches in the marketplace.

Motivated, self-learning, entrepreneurial workers, empowered by and collaborating through new tools, apply their knowledge and creativity to create value. Conditions may warrant a solid structure that tightly bonds molecules together. More likely, conditions will require more dynamic relationships among molecules causing them to cluster in teams, as in liquid crystals, or even to move more freely, as in liquids. The capacity for new relationships is profoundly increased through the new infrastructure.

There is still a role for the organization to provide a base structure for such molecular activity, but it is a far cry from the old hierarchy.[7]

THEME 5: Integration/Internetworking

'The new economy is a network economy, integrating molecules into clusters.'

The new technology networks enable small companies to overcome the main advantage of large companies - economies of scale and access to resources. At the same time, these smaller companies are not burdened with the main disadvantages of large firms - deadened bureaucracy, stifling hierarchy and the inability to change. As larger companies disaggregate - become clusters of smaller molecules that can work well together - they gain the advantages of agility, autonomy, and flexibility.

> The Internetworked Enterprise will be a far-reaching extension of the virtual corporation because there will be access to external business partners, constant reconfiguration of business relationships and a dramatic increase in outsourcing. The Internetworked Enterprise will behave like the Internet, where everyone can participate and the total effort is greater than the sum of its parts.[8]

> We will see the rise of the internetworked business, internetworked government, internetworked learning and internetworked health care to name a few.[9]

The overall economy will act in the same way. Networks of networks along the Internet are beginning to break down walls among suppliers, customers, affinity groups, and competitors.

THEME 6: Disintermediation

Middleman functions between producers and consumers are being eliminated through digital networks. These groups need to discover new opportunities.

1. Musicians will not need recording companies.
2. Food producers can sell direct to consumers.
3. Hotels won't need travel agents.
4. Manufacturers can sell direct. (i.e., other services - Black and Decker offers videos on how to do home repairs.)

Summit Travel of North Carolina offers a software program for helping people make their own reservations on the Internet. Each reservation brings them five percent.

THEME 7: Convergence

In the new economy, the dominant economic sector is being created by three converging industries that, in turn, provide the infrastructure for wealth creation by all sectors.

The dominant sector in the new economy is the **new media**, which are products of the convergence of the computing, communications and content industries. (Entertainment companies, broadcast networks and publishers). The more successful companies are those with a background in software, services, computer-based content, and digital telecommunications.

The recent marriage between Gates, Disney, Eisner and Spielberg are an example of how content, computing and communications come together.

THEME 8: Innovation

The new economy is an innovation-based economy. Build obsolescence into your own products (Microsoft). If you don't do it, someone else will! *Windows '95* made the best selling software of all time, MS-*DOS* (its own product), obsolete.

The key driver of the new economy is innovation and a continued renewal of products, systems, processes, marketing and people.

Some examples of an innovation-driven company include:
Product life cycles collapsing (HP Way).
Sony introducing 5,000 new products in one year.
Nucor Steel - reinventing the process for making steel.
Rubbermaid into continuous innovation - the constant generation of new products and the regeneration of old ones.

Growth comes from small- and medium-sized businesses in which needs are primarily educational.

> What's required are educational systems that teach and motivate students to learn and to be creative, rather than recall information. Governments and regulatory frameworks must help to liberate the human spirit for invention and creation, rather than acting as a bureaucratic brake on change and breakthrough.[10]

Given the pace of change and complexity of markets, customers often cannot articulate their needs. You must innovate beyond what your markets can imagine. You must understand the needs of your customer's customer. Organizations need a deep-seated and pervasive comprehension of emerging technologies. And you need a climate in which risk taking is not punished, creativity can flourish, and human imagination can soar.

THEME 9: Prosumption

In the new economy, the gap between consumers and producers blurs.

Consumers become involved in the production process. Configure a kitchen together with the salesperson on the computer at a building supply depot.

As the information and knowledge content of products and services grows, enterprises will shift from being only consumers of information and technology to the point at which they are info tech producers.

Theme 10: Immediacy

In a 'bit' driven economy, immediacy becomes a key driver and variable in economic activity and business success.

In 1990, automobiles took six years from concept to production. Today, it takes two years. Most of Hewlett Packard's revenue comes from products that didn't exist a year ago.

The new enterprise is 'real time'. Customer orders arrive electronically and are instantly processed, corresponding invoices are sent electronically and databases are updated.

THEME 11: Globalization

1. Knowledge knows no boundaries.
2. Global customers demand global products.
3. Cost advantages are exploited globally.
4. New economic regions blur boundaries.

Globalization is both chicken and egg. It is driven by the new technology, as well as being the driver of this new technology.

Networks enable smaller firms to collaborate in achieving economies of scale. Software development takes place on networks independent of location. Technology is eliminating the 'place' in workplace. Home may be where the heart is, but, increasingly, the office is anywhere a head can be connected.

More than 100 million phone calls are completed every hour on the hour (Editor note: accurate as of the date of writing, it has likely increased many times since then), using 300 million access lines the world over and the number of calls tripled in a few short years.

> The entire globe is now tied together in a single electronic market moving at the speed of light. There is no place to hide. [11]

THEME 12: Discordance

Unprecedented social issues are beginning to arise, potentially causing massive trauma and conflict.

> As tectonic shifts in most aspects of human existence clash with old cultures, significant social conflict will tear at the fabric of structures and institutions. [12]

There is a shift away from the power of the nation state.

There is a concurrent trend toward self-employment and the creation of small knowledge-based industries providing work on a contract basis. Thus, there is a shift from the production floor to the mindset of the knowledge worker who creates value.

Knowledge workers require motivation and trusting team relationships in order to be effective.

In the new economy, learning will be provided more and more by the private sector. This is because work and learning is the same for most of knowledge workers. Moreover, traditional educational institutions fail to provide what is needed by the economy. There is a great opportunity for learning products and services. **Education needs to undergo a transformation.** [13]

In summary, today's new network economy demands that structures, systems and people must reflect the needs of the nanosecond marketplace. Unlike the mechanistic structures of the past, today's structures need to provide the energy to create, to be flexible, and to include highly motivated people who not only understand the customers' beliefs and values, but their strategic and psychological needs. Thus, who the customer is and what he or she values, is the driving force behind the creation of an effective organization.

PEOPLE: TRANSCENDING EVOLUTION'S PURPOSE

To say we are evolved to serve the interests of our genes in no way suggests that we are obliged to serve them. Evolution is surely most deterministic for those still unaware of it.

(Richard D. Alexander, The Biology of Moral Systems, 1987)

If we are truly interested in changing our present reality in both our personal and organizational lives, we need to grasp the full meaning of evolution's purpose. Like Asterope on her Hero's Journey, learning all you can about yourself and others is the first step in deciphering your own potential and meaning in life. By understanding the mechanisms that have brought us to where we are as a species and our inherent capacity for both differentiation and integration, we can more clearly see the path that nature has created for us.

As a species, humans have undergone the same transitions through time that every other species has had to face. Through the process of natural selection, certain physical, mental and behavioural characteristics have been passed from generation to generation, while others were dropped from the gene pool. The occasional genetic mutation caused further variability. As these genes recombined in each successive generation, new potential was created. Strong genes and gene combinations, which promoted reproduction and survival, were more likely to be 'selected' and passed on to offspring.

Although these universal forces of selection created Homo sapiens, we are now in a state of evolution that no other species has ever reached. We are conscious of ourselves and our potential to the point that we can transcend these forces and define a new path for our future.

Post_Darwinist Richard Dawkins, author of 'The Selfish Gene', and one of the world's leading authorities in the field of evolution, points out that although we are survival machines, programmed to preserve our genes, we have an opportunity to transcend our genetic *blueprint.* **We are not merely designed to adapt to change,**

we are capable of creating change. Nature has provided us with surplus genes, allowing us an opportunity to break out of our current self-imposed boundaries. Dawkins calls this surplus 'massive redundancy' and points to the generation of new ideas as an example of this potential. *Creativity has become the thinking process that leads to innovation, which drives us away from the present reality towards achievement of a compelling vision of the future.*

Dawkins has coined the phrase 'memes' as a cognitive analogy to genes, to describe how ideas, intellectual property, songs, fashion, etc. are transmitted from one generation to another. People like Confucius, Socrates, Plato, Gandhi, Moses, Christ and Mohammed are examples of individuals whose ideas have survived the test of time, just as genes carry physical and behavioural information through the ages.

> Memes should be regarded as living structures, not just metaphorically, but technically. When you plant a fertile meme in my mind, you literally parasitize my brain, turning it into a vehicle for the memes propagation in just the way that a virus may parasitize the genetic mechanism of a host cell.[14]

The theory of memes shows that human evolution is a product of more than just the blending of genetic material. Cultural, personal, and historical information also influence our behaviour through the transmission of ideas over time. *Evolution cannot be limited to the adaptation of organisms to their environment because the environment itself is being influenced by a network of living systems capable of both adaptation and creativity*. Physicist Fritjof Capra has called this a dance of competition and co-operation, creation and mutual adaptation.

Biologist Lynn Margulis points out that creativity is expressed through mutation, trading of genes or memes, and symbiosis (networks). These interrelationships, however, are shaped by the process of natural selection (adaptation leading to increased diversity). *To extend this analogy to our own creativity, we can say that when we combine our unique talents (mutations) in a domain that recognizes the important contribution of these talents (networks), we create a higher order in society (evolution).*

The story of Asterope on her journey to self-discovery shows that each individual has unique abilities that they must discover. This differentiation among people ensures that creativity is always possible. But, like Asterope, most of us have an ingrained desire to interact with people and to share our differentiation within a group, leading to integration of all our unique ideas and skills.

There are many examples of how we use our integration and differentiation in life and, particularly, in our business endeavours. In a study of the Niagara Cottage Wine Industry (Luczkiw, 1995), successful growth and evolution of this emerging trade was found to be dependent upon creation of innovative products (differentiation) and exploitation of emerging opportunities. While these were critical factors of success that led to global recognition of this industry, it was the cooperation (integration) of winery owners and trades people that made this success possible. Differentiation and integration are only part of the equation of the successful evolution of the industry. In the previous wine industry example, it is the creativity caused by differentiation and integration that leads to new products and services (mutation in the established industry code). The network that was established determined their commercial viability and took the industry to a new level (evolution).

UNDERSTANDING THE WORKINGS OF OUR BRAIN/MIND

Understanding the natural organization of the brain provides the key to transforming the hierarchical/mechanistic and reductionist mindset, allowing us to accept a more holistic and ecological framework for life and business. Before we can begin to consider the workings of our mind (software), we need to become more acquainted with the physical structure of our brain (hardware).

The brain you are born with has over 200 billion cells called 'neurons' all tucked neatly into the skull. The skull is soft and pliant at birth, not only to ease your entry into this world through the birth canal, but also to accommodate the rapid increase in the size of your brain's outer layer during the first two years of life. This increase occurs not from the addition of neurons, but from the development of many connections between the brain cells. *As you take in information, more and more of these connections are made, thus increasing the surface area of your cerebral cortex.* By the time you reach adulthood, this expanding layer would be two and a half feet square if you were to spread it out like a tablecloth.

HOW THE BRAIN WORKS

Research into the physical structures of our brain and the workings of its software, our mind, points to distinct differences between individuals, both from a genetic and cultural perspective. The brain records your every thought throughout your life, and the resulting topography is different for each one of us. It has been demonstrated that when we make a decision to think a particular thought, our brain's structure actually changes. In other words, what you do with your brain determines how it will actually look.

Dr. Gary Lynch, a psychobiologist at the University of California, Irvine, studied slices of cells taken from Einstein's brain. He found that Einstein had an inordinate amount of glial cells in the region of the brain where associations and connections are established. Lynch determined that *new learning physically alters the brain leaving a biological trail, whether it is learning a new word or the conceptualization of an idea.* Messages pass between the neurons over nerve fibres called *'axons'* and *'dendrites'.* When thought occurs, as in a problem-solving situation, a tiny electrical spark forces the chemicals sodium and potassium into the void between the neurons. The bridge they form is called a synapse. With every message sent, a slight trace of these chemicals is left. With repeated crossings, the thought becomes established and easy to slide into, but difficult to alter (patterns). *Thus, when we seek to change our thinking, we face not only mental challenges, but physical ones, as well.*

Because our brains are more complex than animals, we can consciously change ourselves and our environment. We are capable of increasing our personal flexibility by learning new ways of doing things, and by meeting new challenges. We have an incredible array of abilities, not only to manipulate our environment, but also to control what we think and do.

THE TRIUNE BRAIN

Dr. Paul Maclean in his "Triune Brain Theory" states that, over time, our brain formed separate, but related, layers that made different contributions to our thinking abilities in order to meet the challenges of the environment. The **first layer** is found deep in our skull and rests on top of the brain stem. This is the '*reptilian brain*' and **it controls respiration and other automatic functions**. When you are anxious, this primitive part of your brain sends messages to speed up blood flow, heart rate, muscle tension, and brain waves - the fight or flight response. This is the layer that is responsible for causing stress disorders in men and women. *The reptilian brain has no memory; it is instinctual and reflexive.* This part of the brain is also the source of our striving instincts as identified by Kathy Kolbe in her research into conation. Recent evidence, however, also seems to point to the **frontal lobes as a source of some of our instincts**.

The middle layer of the brain, or 'Limbic System' *is more sophisticated.* It enables you to make the fine distinctions that help you recognize that which is yours *(i.e. your car, wife, friends, etc.)* This layer also enables you to **devise ingenious survival techniques** such as letting your boss win every golf game he plays with you, even though you happen to have a scratch handicap.

As Daniel Goleman pointed out in 'Emotional Intelligence', this part of the brain plays a pivotal role in *expression of feelings and is the source of our passion that leads to action. More importantly, it is the limbic system that also functions as the critical switching system for incoming sensory data. It decides what information gets into your cortex.*

The cortex, found in developed humans, then covers both of these remnants from prehistoric times. It is the area where new learning takes place; where you process your own view of the environment and invent ways of dealing with it. This area consists of over 200 billion neurons, and besides performing cognitive functions, helps us to make needed connections in the process of generating new combinations of ideas.

As the brain evolved, the cortex and limbic parts became divided into two distinct hemispheres, the *Left Brain* and the *Right Brain.* In the early 1960's, Nobel Prize Winner Dr. Robert Sperry, a neuroscientist, and his team determined that the *two sides of the brain perform special and different functions* which are refined each time we respond to change and challenges. In a series of experiments with split-brain patients, they found the following: In right-handed people, the right side of the brain controls the left side of the body and processes information in an emotional way, while the left side of the brain controls the right side of the body and is more specific and logical in its processing.

More recent research by Ned Herrmann (HBDI) and others showed that *most of us tend to use one side of the brain more than the other, and that we have a 'cerebral dominance' or a specialized way of working, communicating, playing and behaving.* In most of us, the dexterity required for writing rests in the right side of our brain, but we use the left side to select the most appropriate words.

While the concept of using a stick as a tool sprung from the reptilian and limbic part of the brain; refining the tool concept to become a circuit board was accomplished in the newer part of the brain, the cortex. The cortex enabled people to remember, plan, invent and to communicate new ideas.

Since Sperry's discoveries, new evidence seems to suggest that given the non-solid, energetic nature of the universe, it is unlikely that only one part of the brain could house all of our creativity, despite the fact that most of us have a greater tendency towards creativity in the right hemisphere. **One thing is certain; everyone has a creative side.**

There are four distinct differences that make the human brain superior to that of other living creatures:

1. It has the most convoluted surface, indicating higher levels of memory and learning.
2. It has the most clearly divided hemispheres, showing the highest level of specialization and sophistication.
3. It has the greatest brain to body weight ratio, signifying the importance of thinking to our survival.
4. It has the most complex set of frontal lobes of all of the world's animals. It may be an indication that we are growing most tissues in the area where planning and innovation takes place.

Our human brain does not have a structure that is devoted to perception (how we see the world). Psychologists have segmented the human mind in a manner that includes thinking, feeling and perceiving. Although this is useful in understanding how these three faculties work and relate to one another, they do not alone tell the whole story. We also need to add our striving instincts (Kathy Kolbe's action modes) to the picture. Although Ned Herrmann has provided us with an integrated model of how the various parts of the brain work, we need to understand how our thoughts and emotions combine to provide us with our view of the world. It is interesting to note that our perceptions are shaped more by our emotions, which seem to direct what enters into our cognitive (thinking) domain. Our perception also takes into account what we see, hear, and smell. These are separate classes of emotion that are found in distinct neural systems that have evolved to fulfill distinct needs. Thus, we use different emotions when we seek pleasure than those used when we flee from a wild bear.

Joseph LeDoux points out that these emotional responses in people occur, for the most part, unconsciously. This fits Freud's analysis of consciousness as being only the tip of the proverbial mental iceberg. Thus, our actions are, for the most part, unconsciously driven, programmed by our genetic blueprint and cultural learning. Libet and Feinstein, two neuroscientists, discovered in controlled experiments that our body began to react to events prior to our conscious awareness of them. **This is why it is so critical for every one of us to become aware of the structural and situational realities of our human brain/mind.**

LeDoux further demonstrates that emotions can flood our consciousness. The wiring in our brain, at this point in our evolution, is such that the connectors from the emotional systems to the cognitive systems are stronger than those coming from the cognitive side. Once these emotions manifest themselves, they become a powerful force in determining and shaping our behaviours. In fact, they can take a thought we have and help drive it into the external environment, where we may connect with people and events that allow us to create new possibilities, identify opportunities and exploit niches in the external environment.

Until recently, people viewed the brain as an extension of the central nervous system based on the principles of electrical communication. Only in the last few decades have we begun to develop instruments that observe the brain as a chemical process. Prior to discoveries of brain peptides in the 1970's, it was thought that neurotransmitters were the sole source of carrying messages as they jumped from one neuron to another across a synapse. Peptides, on the other hand, move through cellular structures swept along in the blood and the cerebrospinal fluid. As they travel long distances, complex and fundamental changes occur in the cells whose receptors they lock into. In light of more recent discoveries in the 1980's, these receptors and ligands, as they are called, have become known as "information molecules", the basic communication unit used by cells to communicate with one another throughout the organism. This process of chemical integration between structure and system ensures the organism's smooth operation.

The frontal cortex of the human brain contains the structural, systemic and chemical elements that differentiate us from other living species. Located just behind our forehead, it houses our higher cognitive functions that include our thinking and organizing capabilities, as well as our capacity to create compelling visions of the future. By exercising and experiencing these capabilities, we influence our will to act, releasing endorphins in the process. While this frontal cortex helps us determine our uniqueness and differentiation, it is dependent upon the flow of peptides of emotion through the psychosomatic networks. This flow of emotion is influenced by our behaviour. If our emotions become blocked, blood flow becomes constricted, depriving the frontal cortex of its essential nourishment and impacting upon our capacity to make informed decisions.

According to Candace Pert (a researcher in the field of biochemistry), our blood flow is regulated by emotional peptides, which signal receptors on blood vessels, influencing the quantity and speed of blood flow from nanosecond to nanosecond. In order to ensure our ability to remain conscious of our actions, sufficient amounts of blood flow carrying glucose to the brain becomes a necessity. Pert was responsible for the discovery of what is known as an opiate receptor. This discovery has influenced a number of fields of study with profound impact on theories of human behaviour, biology, and social psychology. The opiate receptor is what Pert describes as an emotion molecule, which is found on the surface of the body and on the brain. A given nerve cell (neuron) may have millions of receptors on its surface.

Receptors function basically as sensors, much the same as our eyes, ears, nose, skin and tongue. They seek to pick up the right chemical combinations in order to bond with them. This is what Pert describes as **sex at the molecular level.** The chemical element (or peptide) that attaches itself to the receptor is called a ligand. It literally tickles the molecule, causing it to change its shape as new information enters the cell. Having received the message, the cell changes the direction of biochemical events, influencing a spur of activity, which could include the manufacture of new proteins, division of cells, opening and closing of channels, or creation/dissipation of energy. In other words, the life of the cell is determined by this interaction between ligands and receptors, leading to physical and behavioural change. The cell acts as the engine that pilots life, while the receptors are the buttons on the control panel, and the ligand is the finger that actually pushes the button.

Our capabilities cause us to be curious, excitable, gregarious animals who simply must tinker with the environment. In turn, the altered environment sends back stimulating experiences. *Thus, we perpetuate and thrive on constant stimulation and change*.

In the final analysis, what this suggests is that our attitude not only determines how we perceive events, but influences the physical and systemic processes in our bodies. If we are positive about the challenges we face, we release opiates that bathe our cells with feelings of exhilaration and joy. On the other hand, negative attitudes have a tendency to suppress the opiates, leading to opposite results.

How we think not only helps us to explore future challenges and possibilities, but also serves to identify our preferences. Pioneering research, conducted by Howard Gardiner, has identified at least eight intelligences that we as a human race possess. Our school system and society, as a whole, has focussed primarily on two of them. Understanding that not everyone is **linguistically** or **mathematically** gifted, Gardiner has focussed on six other intelligences that need to be nurtured in today's environment: kinaesthetic, musical, spatial, intrapersonal, interpersonal and environmental. The key is that learning needs to be individualized to the point that the traditional 3 R's become relevant through interaction with these intelligences.

The fact that scientists who study the cognitive domain rarely compare notes with those who study human emotion adds to the challenge of trying to get the big picture. **Our mind is more than something that Artificial Intelligence can replicate. It is a combination of four human faculties that generally act unconsciously in helping us to make our way in this world.**

- Conation (instinct)
- Cognation (thinking)
- Affect (action)
- Perception (sensing)

Once we discover how our brain/mind works, then we can consciously create and shape a compelling future for ourselves.

Dr. Terry Brandt reports that the number of thoughts generated inside our brain exceeds by hundreds of times the number of sensory inputs we register. He can actually measure the fact that we generate more thoughts inside our own brain than we get input from the environment. This evidence confirms that we see and hear what we want to see. In essence, we create our own reality.

THE HOLOGRAPHIC BRAIN

As already discussed, modern physics view the universe as a vast inseparable web of dynamic activity. Not only is it constantly changing, but it is living nature affecting everything, everywhere. At its most basic level, the universe is a whole, undifferentiated force of energy that transcends everything. According to theories of quantum mechanics, everything is part of a pattern that is in constant motion. Our universe is a dynamic living system, much like ourselves. The human brain is a hologram interpreting a holographic universe. The theories that led to the development of the hologram were formulated by Nobel Laureate Dennis Gabor, who *identified a hologram as an entity, where the whole is contained in every one of the parts*. In the same manner, an individual's entire genetic imprint is contained in each and every body cell (except sex cells). If one were to shatter a holographic plate, each of the parts would reveal the whole image.

The main architects behind this idea of a holographic universe were David Bohm, a quantum physicist, and Karl Pribram, a neurophysiologist at Stanford University. Working in two different fields of science, they reached similar conclusions. The holographic model provided answers to the challenges they both faced. Both concluded that our thinking was ultimately connected to the physical world.

In early experiments, Karl Pribram discovered that when large portions of brains were destroyed in animals, they could still carry out learned activities; although at a somewhat impaired level. This led Pribram to posit *"How could specific learning be transmitted throughout the brain?'* His inspiration came from the relationships between physical and mathematical bases of holograms.

Pribram argued that the brain operates as a holographic plate with a full three-dimensional image. **Throughout the brain, interference patterns operate like holograms to represent memory traces and interactions with the environment, which would explain the lack of memory loss in damaged brains.** This led Pribram to a deeper question: *"If the brain puts together the internal memory frequencies with the new external experiential frequencies, who is interpreting the resulting holograms?"* In other words, *"Who experiences our experiences?"* Michael

Gazzaniga, a protégé of Roger Sperry, has identified a region called the 'interpreter' in the brain, which seems to house this function.

David Bohm, a contemporary of Einstein, argued that the entire world has holographic properties and that each person is one fragment. As Bohm points out, there is an implicate order out there and an infinite sea of energy, and this unfolds to form space, time and matter. This implicate order that you can look at physically can also be felt internally as consciousness, or 'essence'. **Thought is a real factor in the world**.

Biologist Rupert Sheldrake has taken David Bohm's and his contemporaries' theories of physics and integrated them into the fields of biology and psychology. His thesis points to random chance events (luck) as being the result of creative manifestations. The new physicists indicate that tremendous energy resources exist within us and that we unite with existing energy patterns in the universe. Sheldrake builds a case for the existence of what he calls morphogenic fields, or invisible organizing structures, that mold or shape things like crystals, plants and animals, also having an organizing effect on behaviour. He posits that these morphogenic fields contain influences from all of history and evolution. This helps explain the 'lucky factor' that often identifies the 'opportunity' in both a business and non-business environment (luck is where preparation meets opportunity). Sheldrake points out that when you discover your unique sense of creativity, you are tuning in to these morphogenic fields of similar thoughts and biological structures (other people or events). He compares this to a television receiving invisible signals from the television station. In the same manner, we can tune in to these signals if we dial the right frequency.

Scientific evidence today confirms that each of us has free access to the accumulated wisdom, knowledge and creativity from all ages and corners of the world. The Internet is merely a small piece of this big picture. More and more, scientific evidence points to creativity as the process that turns the chaos in our lives into a higher order, as we continue to grow. It is our creativity that leads us to a higher level of order.

Nobel Laureate Ilya Prigogine, a physical chemist by profession, points out that human beings are open systems, or dissipative structures. Not only do we focus our energies in predetermined directions, we are also complex in the sense that we contain a myriad of networks and energy flows. In the scientific sense, we are never in the state of equilibrium, but on the edge of order and chaos (explicate order). It is this instability that leads to creative responses. Anything that increases stress on the system leads to a higher level of achievement. Instead of breaking down, you break through into a higher level of thinking and a higher state of mind.

Experimental evidence supporting Prigogine's theories has shown that molecules cooperate in vast patterns in reaction to a new challenge (i.e. bacteria). When placed in a medium that would normally kill them, they develop new interactions that enable them to survive at this higher level. Prigogine's work extends to humans. His findings point to a scientific basis for creativity in our lives. When you surrender to your own unique creative source, you tune in this morphed resonance - the communication across time and space via morphogenic fields between similar biological structures or thoughts. This is not unlike Asterope's growing creativity as she began to connect with others along her route or an entrepreneur who drives their enterprise by connecting with their creative side.

Many of today's scientific breakthroughs are also revelations in a profound spiritual sense. By implying that each person possesses an invisible creative source, science goes beyond accepting the existence of consciousness. It also compels us to awaken and transform ourselves to become one with the gifts that we bring into this world.

In the late 1970's, Robert G. John, Dean of the School of Engineering and Applied Sciences at Princeton University, found, after thousands of controlled experiments, sufficient evidence to clearly demonstrate the mind's ability to directly influence physical reality.

Our consciousness is an energy force that interacts with this physical world. Events are affected by what we desire, fear, imagine, and visualize, demonstrating how an image held in the mind can become real. If we are consciously aware that we are part of an open and dynamic universe, our minds play a decisive role in constructing reality, allowing us to live more creatively and energetically. Management guru, Peter Drucker's widely quoted insight that "the best way to predict the future is to create it", now has a great deal of scientific support behind it.

As human beings, we live simultaneously in two separate worlds:

1. Our inner world of attitudes, emotions and thoughts (intrinsic), and
2. An external world of events, people, places and things (extrinsic).

Because we are not conscious of their separate existence, we allow ourselves to be dominated by the outer world of appearances and we use the inner world as a mirror for what happens to us. *Our inner world constantly reacts to this external world and we never experience our potential. You can only change your reality when you cease reacting to this outer world.* Your inner consciousness is a powerful force whose influence is felt in every aspect of your life. It is the most important part of who you are, and is the determinant of your success or failure.

You need to be aware, first and foremost, that your emotions determine what you choose to think about. As a consequence, you become what you think. **Your thinking induces your energy force.** The more the thought is repeated, the more energy and power it generates and the more readily it manifests itself. *Thoughts need to be concentrated in order to derive the needed energy to interact effectively in the external environment,* in much the same way that a magnifying glass concentrates the sun's rays on a sheet of paper. Deeply held beliefs, fears, hopes, worries, attitudes, and desires affect you, others and your environment. In most cases, we go through life paying little attention to how we think, let alone all those other everyday chores and challenges we face.

Considering we think thousands of thoughts every day, we need to become more conscious of what direction we want to focus these thoughts.

SYSTEMS THINKING: CONNECTING OUR "SELF" WITH THE EXTERNAL ENVIRONMENT

As already discussed, this world of ours is a living system, full of energy. Living systems are integrated wholes whose properties cannot be reduced to smaller parts. Thus, every thought you have influences, and is influenced by, the system. You create your reality through your thoughts. When a system is dissected into separate parts, their systemic properties are destroyed. *Systems thinking is contextual in that explanations are based on interactions with the external environment.* Relationships are primary and objects are considered secondary. *Organic networks replace knowledge as building blocks. When we perceive reality as a network of relationships, our globe is seen as a dynamic web of interrelated events.*

Different system levels demonstrate distinct levels of complexity. (The more complex the structure, the greater the chance of survival.) In the case of human relationships, complexity is defined as the combination of differentiation and integration where each person pursues their individuality, while sharing their uniqueness with others in the community. Bill Gates and Microsoft have reached their state of complexity by creating innovations such as Windows and making them available to consumers and software developers. In the field of evolutionary economics, this is known as the 'law of increasing returns' and 'lock-in', as previously discussed.

Living systems cannot be understood on the basis of analysis. The parts of the system can only be understood within the context of the whole. An organizational vision takes on meaning that compels individuals to pursue their uniqueness within its contextual framework. **No one can predict the bumps, twists and turns of the journey, but the vision created by leaders and shared and supported by the community creates the needed focus towards its achievement.**

Nature is an interconnected network of relationships in which the identification of specific patterns as objects depends on the human observer and the process of knowing. As Werner Heisenberg pointed out more than 70 years ago, "What we observe is not nature itself, but nature exposed to our method of questioning". These relationships form a network of concepts and models, none of which is any more fundamental than the others. Within this reality, all scientific concepts and theories are limited and approximate. Science can never provide a complete and definite understanding. As a result, no matter how many connections we undertake, we will always leave others out.

HUMAN BEINGS AS LIVING SYSTEMS

"Human organisms are endowed from the very beginning with a spirited passion for making choices which our social mind can use to build rational behaviour." (Damasio)

Firstly, we are autonomous beings, shaped by our own history of structural change. Secondly, we are conscious beings aware of who we are and what makes us unique. Thirdly, we do not operate in a vacuum - we are made up of bundles of relationships. Fourthly, individuality and autonomy need not imply separateness and independence. *They are our energy force that allows our uniqueness and differentiation to seek out others in order that we may create new possibilities, identify potential opportunities and exploit emerging niches.*

As human beings, we are complex living organisms. Our brains, as organisms in and of themselves, consist of multiple components, each with distinct working regions. Each part of the brain consists of biological tissues, made up of cells, which, in turn, are part of the molecular structure. As this living organism is constantly changing, it is "assuming a succession of states, each defined by varied patterns of on-going activity in all of its components" (Domasio, 2005[15] 4, p.87)

Antonio Domasio (author of 'Descartes Error' and professor of neurosciences at Iowa State University) likens the brain to a large busy airport terminal. "The brain and the body are **indissociably** integrated by mutually targeted biochemical and neural circuits"(ibid, p.87). Nearly every part of our body can send signals to the brain via the peripheral nerves. They enter via the reptilian part of the brain and then carry on into the limbic and cortex. Chemical substances from bodily reactions reach the brain through the bloodstream, influencing the brain's operation by directly activating special regions. The brain also acts on the body by means of the nervous system, as well as by manufacturing chemical substances and releasing them through the bloodstream.

Knowledge recall, in the form of images, comes from many regions of the brain. While it appears that everything comes together at a single location, recent evidence suggests that this is not the case. As Domasio points out, "probably the relative simultaneity of activity at different sites binds the separate parts of the mind together" (p. 84). Domasio goes on to say that the images over which we reason must not only be in focus through our ability to direct attention at them, but must also be held actively in the mind by our highly complex memory system. This is consistent with findings of Mikaly Csiksentmilakyi (The Evolution of Self).

As individuals, we require broad-based knowledge and reasoning strategies in order to operate within such an uncertain environment. While this knowledge includes a wide variety of information about our external environment, it must also include an understanding of the mechanisms related to the regulation of the organism, as a whole. Emotions are part and parcel of the neural machinery for biological regulation whose core consists of homeostatic controls, drives and instincts.

This living systems approach to understanding our role and ability in life has been adopted by many successful organizations. On the other hand, the education that most of us received was designed to prepare us to take our place within a bureaucracy or on the assembly line. Schools paid lip service to promoting originality and independent thinking, while training us to be good at following the rules and anticipating the requirements of authority. Those who succeeded in the hierarchical structures were reluctant to give up their hard won sense of control. As a result, little has changed in the organization of the school system from kindergarten through to the post-secondary level. Although these institutions have begun to use and continue to echo the words enterprise and living systems, they are not yet capable of instilling these new entrepreneurial molecular structures into what remains a mechanistic/reductionist environment. The existing structures need to embody the principles of knowledge creation, creativity and innovation, and complex networks so that we create the tension necessary to bring about change.

ECOSYSTEMS: CONNECTING EVERYONE AND EVERYTHING IN TODAY'S GLOBAL VILLAGE

Dawkins stated that we are survival machines programmed to preserve the selfish units known as genes. Just like a gangster in an organized criminal gang, a successful gene is expected to be ruthless and selfish. There are, however, occasions when selfish genes behave altruistically, i.e. when they need to co-operate with one another to replicate themselves and make the needed proteins, as in the case of DNA. Genes must compete for their place in the chromosomes of a future generation, in order to achieve their ultimate goal of replication and survival.

How, then, can we expect human beings to behave differently? After all, don't we, by and large, follow the dictates of our genes? In his book, *Not In Our Genes*, Richard C. Lewontin points out that, in spite of the selfishness of our genes, we have been provided with mental, physical and vocal attributes, along with a wide range of flexibility within these genetic structures. Our biological determinants have given us the freedom to co-create and re-create our psychological and physical environment. Our individuality is shaped by interaction with a multiplicity of intersecting, causal relationships and connections, while special genetic processes, such as reshuffling, mutation and natural selection, enhance our reproductive capabilities.

The purpose of natural selection has been broadened to include the process of kin selection. This can be demonstrated in ant colonies, as well as in the history of human evolution. The immediate family becomes a model for attempts to sacrifice oneself for the growth of the future generation and, in the process, the propagation of selfish genes is achieved.

These altruistic acts performed by members of the immediate family are largely **culturally determined.** Culture has been defined by Geert Hofstede as the collective programming of the mind that distinguishes members of one group of people from another. It requires the training and refining of the mind and manifests itself through our emotional faculties, having evolved through our genes. Our genetic structures then program our mental faculties in a manner that determines how we react to our environment.

As social beings, people have long since discovered that they cannot just selfishly pursue their individual needs. When they recognize that through co-operation they can create new possibilities that benefit them, they begin to explore other scenarios. Society offers other benefits in the form of safety nets that ensure material and personal survival in difficult times. Thus, as human beings, our own development is the result of many interacting and intersecting causes. Our actions become our own, independent and unrestrained by any gene or cultural meme.

> Our biology has made us into creatures who are constantly recreating our own psychic and material environments, and whose individual lives are the outcomes of an extraordinary multiplicity of intersecting causal pathways. Thus, it is our biology that makes us free.[16]

Game Theory was developed for the purpose of understanding the evolution of human behaviour, ranging from interspecies symbiosis to territoriality in the animal kingdom. The point of this comparison is to show how the success of our own species can be enhanced through cooperation. These experiments have been expanded in an age of high-speed computers and are now used for a variety of purposes.

One of the pioneers in the field, Robert Axelrod, has studied the evolution of co-operation. By devising a series of simulations, he was able to devise behavioural strategies in ongoing computer tournaments. In his book, *The Evolution of Co-operation*, (Basic Books, 1984), Axelrod asked, "Under what conditions will co-operation emerge in a world of egotists without central authority?" - a question not easily answered. Axelrod also pointed out a number of critical human factors that included the following:

1. People are not angels.
2. People look after themselves and their own first.

However, cooperation does occur in our society, and, in fact, our success is dependent upon it. The question still remains: If each person has an incentive to be selfish and our genetic blueprint further enhances this behaviour, how does cooperation ever develop?

This is particularly relevant in today's explosive global environment, where individuals and nations operate without any central authority. If one country were to remove its trade barriers, it could seriously damage its domestic economy if the other countries failed to reciprocate. Alternatively, retaining its trade barriers could lead to worse economic performance than if everyone was to collaborate with one another.

As discussed earlier, the law of increasing returns in the field of economics has become the source of the New Economics. It opens the door to collaboration and co-operation among the many agents in the economy. It is based on the principle that if you make your technology available to the widest possible group of individuals, they will benefit by it at the lowest cost. You will also create a dependence on it by external and internal stakeholders, whose success becomes entwined with your innovation. William Gates' Windows format is a dramatic illustration of this economic principle. By making Windows the standard, software writers seeking wide distribution sought to become part of the Window's format. The paradox of the law of increasing returns is its second component, 'lock-in', which inhibits collaboration by providing successful entrants with virtual control of the marketplace. It will take a tremendous leap of ingenuity to unseat the Windows format.

One of the most effective demonstrations of collaboration in action is the Tit for Tat game. Developed by Professor Anatol Rapaport at the University of Toronto, it has become the standard for providing a rationale for why it is important to collaborate. The key element of the game is forgiveness. As long as the other player doesn't act in a selfish manner, you keep being nice to them. If he/she is not nice to you, you reciprocate immediately. You continue to be nice if your opponent has learned his/her lesson from your actions. In all the studies around the globe, it was found that Tit for Tat was successful over a wide range of environments.

"What accounts for Tit for Tat's robust success is its combination of being nice, retaliatory, forgiving and clear. Its niceness prevents it from getting into unnecessary trouble. Its retaliation discourages the other side from persisting whenever defection is tried. Its forgiveness helps restore mutual cooperation. And its clarity makes it intelligible to the other player, thereby eliciting long-term cooperation." (From Gaia to Selfish Gene, p. 131)

For example: Partner A and Partner B have had an ongoing successful business relationship based on trust, with deals sealed with a handshake. Partner B then embarks on a business venture with Partner C, expecting the same rules of trust to apply. However, Partner C goes against a condition in the unwritten contract. Using the Tit for Tat format for success, Partner B has no recourse but to retaliate harshly against Partner C, showing that it is unacceptable behaviour if their relationship is to continue. At the same time, Partner B forgives partner C for the indiscretion and their relationship continues if Partner C chooses to cooperate fully.

Having provided the rationale for the need to collaborate while pursuing your own individuality, we are now ready to approach the issues related to the view that our globe is a giant interconnected whole, where everyone and everything is connected to one another. By accepting this view, we can begin to understand the multitude of connections between individuals within the complexity of the global village.

PASSION: DEVELOPING CONSCIOUSNESS AND CREATIVITY

"The deeper and broader our consciousness of the world becomes, the more complex the layers of processing necessary to obtain that consciousness".

- Derek Buckerton, Language and Species, 1990

In order to become an effective, empowered and self-determining participant in today's rapidly changing, often chaotic and complex global environment, you need to begin a journey to discover your purpose. Asterope, daughter of Atlas, began her quest by leaving the comfort of Olympia. Starting with a clear sense of your inner consciousness and meaning, this complex process involves the union of all your human faculties as you seek to identify challenges and opportunities, which match your individual interests, strengths and talents. By integrating and synthesizing your own uniqueness within the external environment and by creating possibilities that give your life meaning, you begin to discover your purpose and take control of your life.

The process of becoming conscious means becoming aware of those forces that drive us and learning how to act upon those forces to achieve what we desire in life. Each one of us should begin with a personal biography of our self. By reflecting upon those moments that forged our core beliefs, we can determine the forces that have shaped us, and those that give meaning to our lives. Every one of us is a creative being. There are no limits to what we can accomplish, if we believe it to be true. When you have a strong belief in yourself, your most important desires become intentions. Intentions lead to attempts, which, in turn, lead to commitment and action.

As you become conscious, you begin to pay more attention to the flow of your thoughts and direct them towards the achievement of your vision. You must be consistent in focusing on your vision. You may want to create a successful enterprise, but if your consciousness fears the unknown and lives in weakness and worry, how will you ever get the strength to deal with all the challenges of business growth? Merely wanting something to happen, or working eighteen-hour days, will only leave you with your wheels spinning. *You need to begin by changing your thought selection process. This may take time as you first need to reprogram your unconscious, the receptacle of all the limiting beliefs you have gathered over the years.* It is only when you begin replacing them with positive affirmations that you begin increasing your subconscious vocabulary.

Only when you are free to create your own thoughts with a strong focus on a future vision, will you begin to create the needed tension that will drive you from your present reality towards your vision of a future. **By developing a consciousness, your thinking becomes focused on achievement of goals related to your original vision. You discover meaning in life that identifies your purpose, which, in turn, provides you with the needed intrinsic motivation.**

It is not your circumstances and situations that keep you down, but rather your limited belief system. Your reality will change after you have become conscious when you have discovered what really matters. Only then can you begin to focus your thoughts by creating your reality. **No matter what your situation, or how many times you failed in the past, you can change your situation by focusing your thoughts on your vision.**

Your mind is divided up into the conscious, unconsciousness and collective unconscious. Your conscious mind focuses on what you want to create. Your unconscious is the garden that grows the seeds planted by your conscious mind. You can either plant the seeds of your compelling future or those of a limiting belief system. Your unconscious cannot distinguish the good seeds from the weeds - **only your consciousness can**, which means you first must become conscious. *You must become aware of your thinking, change it to reflect what you want to achieve, and then focus it towards the vision you create.* By interacting with others pursuing their uniqueness, you begin to create the needed networks that lead towards the growth of those seeds you planted. Your collective unconscious contains a historical blueprint of the thinking, feeling, and perception of previous generations.

What is true for individuals is also true for organizations. Each person can align their thinking with the meaning, purpose and vision of the organization on the one hand, while pursuing their uniqueness and differentiation on the other.

THROUGH THE LOOKING GLASS: THE PARADOX OF CONSCIOUSNESS

According to Mihaly Csikszentmihalyi, we normally allow a whole series of illusions to stand between ourselves and reality. Built around our genetic instructions, cultural rules, and unbridled desires of the self, these distortions become a source of comfort for us. However, to become truly free, we need to see through these distortions.

The more that is known about how the mind works, the more we realize that the filter through which we experience the world has some peculiar, built-in biases. If we do not understand how these biases work, our thoughts, feelings, perceptions and actions are never truly going to be under conscious control.

This knowledge provides the starting point from which we can build an understanding of our self, identify our interests, strengths and talents, and then proceed to create a personal plan of action that will lead to our self-determination.

CONSCIOUSNESS VS. INTELLIGENCE

To understand the relationship between consciousness and intelligence, let's go back to our comparison of the mind and brain. The mind is what you get when you add up all the parts and functions of the brain and find the result is greater than the sum of these elements. Likewise, intelligence is a measure of the mind's activity, while consciousness (as it relates to self-awareness) is a combination of intelligence and other self-discovery elements that make up our holistic selves.

If the mind is an evolving personal aspect of the human brain, it can only be recognized if we are conscious. Brain and mind may work in parallel, but the mind's software drives the brain in the same way that a pilot steers his plane. It is our conscious actions that can create what has not been created before. Hence, consciousness gives life to the human mind. It also empowers us to become who we want to be and, in effect, transcend our own human evolution. We, indeed, have the power to create our own future.

There is a wide overlap between consciousness and intelligence. Consciousness is the state of awareness during the waking period of our lives, while intelligence refers to the efficiency and the imagination of our mental lives. The higher intellect may actually require conscious and subconscious processing. Philosopher Paul M. Churchland points out the following features of consciousness:

It utilizes short-term memory (working memory).
It is independent of sensory inputs, in that we can think about things not present and imagine unreal things.
It displays steerable attention.
It has the capacity for alternative interpretations of complex or ambiguous data.
It disappears in deep sleep.
It reappears in dreaming.
It contains the contents of several sensory modalities within a single unified experience.

EMERGENCE OF CONSCIOUSNESS

Existing research demonstrates that the richness of the connections we make within our brains determines the complexity, quality and character of our human development. As Professor Susan Greenfield points out, networks are critical to our survival. The degree of stimulation from the environment will determine how connections between neurons will form, leading to the creation of individual memories, which make up the person you are. Memories are the cornerstones of your mind. They are the emergent properties resulting from interactions between the various regions of the brain (including physical, chemical and psychological properties) and the external environment.

When a certain level of complexity is reached, emergent properties, or new behaviours begin to emerge. Think of a noise that triggers an avalanche. *The conditions for an avalanche were reached prior to an event that set it in motion. Behaviours and avalanches have one thing in common. When a certain level of complexity is reached, new emergent behaviours arise.* The expression "we become what we think about" is the result of focusing on what we want to create, and allowing our consciousness to gather all those thoughts and words, such that it will lead to the emerging creation itself. These emergent properties include human consciousness, as well as intelligence and higher mental functions. According to James Trefil, when we have reached this threshold of complexity, just as in the case of the avalanche, our consciousness kicks in.

THE STUDY OF CONSCIOUSNESS

By the middle of the twentieth century, the emerging field of psychology began to focus on the human mind vis-à-vis our actions in the external environment. This became known as the study of human behaviour. The behaviourist school was based on Newton's mechanistic and reductionist models that served to reduce human behaviour to its lowest common denominator (stimulus/response). The alternative model in this era was Freud's model of psychiatry, which focused on the structure of the human mind. This model also relied on Newton's system in the field of biological sciences for answers. Freud concluded that the individual's behaviour was driven by the need to increase pleasure and/or to reduce pain.

By the end of the 1950's, psychology began to take on new approaches and new meaning by integrating principles of quantum physics (replacing Newton's mechanistic model), not only in the fields of physical science, but also in the biological and psychological arenas. **The works of Einstein, Schrödinger, Bohr and Heisenberg were beginning to reshape reductionist thinking with a more ecological and intimate plan of nature, where matter, as the smallest common denominator, was replaced by energy.**

When psychologists began to consider Eastern philosophies along with this emerging scientific paradigm, a new ecological perspective began to emerge that would form the basis of the new psychology. This new psychology became known as the humanistic movement. Led by Abraham Maslow, Viktor Frankl and others, it culminated in **the birth of the human consciousness revolution.** This new movement found Freud's theories too obsessed with the pleasure principles that included sexual desires and began to focus on human perception. **These humanists were influenced by Eastern philosophies where consciousness was studied from within, in a manner consistent with how human beings experience themselves and the world around them.**

According to Psychologist William Stern, in his text 'General Psychology on a Personalistic Basis' (1950), each living being possesses an undifferentiated wholeness with its own character called the persona. Stern stated that the human being could only be understood if the persona became evident. *The persona is the essence of our being.* It is driven towards self-preservation and towards self-development. It is part of a larger world, but is separated from this world by a membrane. This persona is a microcosm that represents body, mind and spirit through a number of distinct characteristics:

1. The persona is goal orientated. We live for as long as possible to realize the development of our potential from our aptitudes and talents.
2. It is conscious of itself. Although consisting of many distinct parts and elements, which are individualized personas themselves, a person perceives herself as a complete "I". In turn, the "I" becomes part of a larger external culture--a structure of structures.
3. It is interdependent with an external world. External elements constantly enter our human self by means of bacteria, food or ideas. Our own ideas

enter our culture. By creating a relationship with the external world, every experience represents another piece of a lifelong dialogue with the world.

4. We are living, but are finite. One day we are living, another day we die. As living beings, we possess a will of our own. Unlike inanimate objects, where causality is measured, human beings possess a will that allows us to work towards achievement of our purpose. As a result of many human beings expressing their individual wills around the globe concurrently and consecutively, the future cannot be predicted in advance.

WHAT IT MEANS TO BE CONSCIOUS

After millions of years of evolution, we have discovered that we possess a self-conscious mind that can think, feel, perceive, act and reflect upon our experiences. With the possible exception of the higher primates and cetaceans, we are the only species to possess this gift. Moreover, it is our need for explanations that separates us from these higher mammals. We call this characteristic *consciousness.*

- Consciousness comes from the Latin term con-scire meaning *that with which we know.* It is a necessity for experience in the same manner as light is for sight. Human consciousness depends greatly on our ability to form and interpret symbolic representations of the outside world. It seems that ability, like seeing, hearing and remembering, is only partly a matter of learning.

- Consciousness is self-existent. Knowing our inner sense of being also frees us from the power grip of our ego. Only when we reach this inner sense of consciousness can we begin to experience the world as it is.

- If we want to discover our essence of being through our meaning, we need first to become conscious. To become conscious, we need to strip away those genetic and cultural determinants that have shaped our thoughts and actions. We need to break past those walls that have hidden our true 'self' from ourselves.

- Antonio Damasio, in *Descartes Error,* describes consciousness as a concept of your own self, something that you construct on the basis of your own biography and a sense of your own future.

- Consciousness can be described as the state of mind that allows us to know our own mind, to think about thinking, and to monitor both ourselves and our environment, in order to turn our dreams into visions and personal achievements.

- *Consciousness* allows us to weigh alternatives, *preventing us from acting in an instinctive/reactive manner.* To be conscious means to be able to direct our specific conscious events (thoughts, feelings, perceptions and actions).

Therefore, consciousness intentionally orders information that comes from the external environment and determines where we choose to direct our attention.

- Consciousness also mirrors our perceptions, telling us what is happening inside and outside ourselves. It reflects these events selectively, shaping these external circumstances and thereby imposing a reality of their own. The sum total of these reflections is our life experience.

The process of becoming conscious means becoming aware of those forces that drive us and discovering how to act upon these forces; how to shape our destiny and how to achieve what we want out of life. By becoming conscious of who we are, why we exist and what and how we need to do in order to achieve and sustain meaning and motivation in our life, we can then begin to take the steps needed to create a compelling vision of our future.

This alignment of our consciousness of self, our meaning and intrinsic motivation helps us to discover our life's purpose. By acting through our striving instincts (conation), we ensure that the vision we create, the mission that we choose, and the goals that we set will lead us to face the challenges of our environment. By pursuing our goals and sharing their outcomes with others, we can achieve the highest state of evolution: *Complexity.*

Thus, we need to become conscious so that we can grow as human beings in both power and competence. To become competent, we need to delve into our inner self to discover what kinds of activities provide us with 'flow' - activities where we lose all track of time and where we use all our senses in 'balanced concentration', working on a challenge that gives us meaning. This is how, by differentiating ourselves and then sharing our outcomes with others, we can truly embark on life's most exciting journey; a journey that includes chaos, complexity and order.

While most people adopt goals based on the needs of health, survival, security, personal interaction, and hard work, there are those who depart from these norms. Super heroes, saints and entrepreneurs create what has not been created before. This is proof that consciousness can be ordered in terms of different goals and intentions. "Each of us has the freedom to control our subjective reality."

The challenge is to use our consciousness to change our thinking so that it reflects the needs of emerging structures and systems in our world today. If we are to become proactive participants, influencing and thriving on chaos and change, we need to embody a different set of enterprising mental models.

DEVELOPING YOUR CONSCIOUSNESS

What **we call our psyche or consciousness is a source of all our accumulated experiences**. This collective consciousness is the source of our energy. This energy becomes a force that begins to seek similar associations, experiences, and patterns in the external environment. This leads to the creation of focused worldviews that help explain the external environment. The challenge, of course, is that we see the present reality in terms of our past experiences. Unfortunately, **the past has little to do with providing us with holistic approaches to deal with future challenges.**

Suffice to say that, through our consciousness, we are the thinker of our own thoughts and thus, we can influence our own actions. However, as Libet and Fernstein have discovered, most of our actions and reactions are unconscious. **This underlies the importance of consciously creating a vision based on our personal purpose, rather than simply on our past experiences.**

With the emergence of cognitive psychology, we begin to discover that human beings possess a tendency to direct attention towards events in the external environment based on our past experiences. Thus, in order for us to act upon signals from the outside world, we need to match them with something that already exists in our mind, placed there by past events and experiences.

Information enters our consciousness either because of our intention to focus **attention** on it or as a result of our biological or social instructions. Driving from home to work each day the same way, you perform complex driving instructions and mental operations in an unconscious manner. It is **attention** that selects the relevant bits of information from the millions of potential combinations, evaluating the situation and selecting the right one. It's like retrieving information from memory storage and bringing it into awareness, comparing information, evaluating, deciding, and so on.

> The mark of a person who is in control of consciousness is the ability to focus attention at will, to be oblivious to distractions, to concentrate for as long as it takes to achieve a goal and not longer.[17]

Attention is the most critical tool we have in improving the quality of our experiences. Air force pilots can discriminate an enemy plane from their own in a fraction of a second. Eskimos discriminate between dozens of types of snow. **Attention** becomes an energy force that guides us through the situations found in the external environment.

According to neurologist David Inguar, we instinctively create action plans and programs for the future. This actively takes place during both our waking hours and while we are asleep. These plans allow us to react to external challenges when they occur by having already played them out in our mind. These *memories of the future* help to sort out the multitude of images entering the brain by assigning degrees of relevance to them. We perceive something as meaningful if it fits with a memory we have already made about an anticipated future.

The act of perception is an active engagement with the external environment. Perception requires a deliberate effort to visit the future in order to develop time paths and options. By discovering ways to develop memories of the future, we ensure that we will succeed in dealing with external challenges when they occur.

THE SELF

The self is one of the constituents of your consciousness. It contains everything that has passed through your consciousness. All memories, experiences, desires, pleasures and pain are found within our consciousness. Most important, your s*elf* represents the hierarchy of goals that you have built up over the years. There is a circular flow in this process with no clear cause and effect.

As Csikszentmihalyi states:

> At one point we are saying the self directs attention; at another, that attention directs itself. In fact, both of these statements are true: consciousness is not strictly a linear system.... Attention shapes the self, and in turn is shaped by it.[18]

Csikszentmihalyi has identified *Flow* as the ultimate experience that leads to achieving a complex state of meaning. It takes place when we are pursuing our vision, totally focussing on our purpose and mission, while sharing these achievements with others. This experience called *Flow* can be found in any situation.

Among the respondents in his studies, Csikszentmihalyi found that one of the most often-mentioned features of this experience is a sense of discovery either of self or the many opportunities that the environment offers.

Most games, sports, artistic performances and religious ceremonies have well-specified goals and rules, so that at any given moment, participants know whether their actions are appropriate or not. Such activities provide flow readily and are intrinsically motivating. In everyday life -- and all too often on the job or in classrooms – the purpose of our activities is not altogether clear and it takes a long time to evaluate how well we are doing. Whenever an activity produces flow, there is a strong tendency for people to repeat it.

THE OUTCOMES OF THE FLOW EXPERIENCE

One becomes interested in an activity either because it was satisfying in the past, one is talented at it or somehow one has attributed value to it. People will not continue to pursue these activities unless they enjoy them or they receive extrinsic rewards for them. Initially, they may undertake these activities because of a need to take risks, seek sensations, etc. However, it is this flow experience that releases endorphins to stimulate the joy of doing it. How we think about something changes the brain's physiology. Thus, knowledge and skill precede *ACTION*.

> Whenever we discover new challenges, we use new skills, and we feel a deep sense of enjoyment. To repeat, we must find even higher challenges, build more sophisticated skills and as we do so, we help the evolution of complexity along its path.[19]

The connection between flow and enjoyment may have been a genetic accident, but once it occurred, it caused individuals to become more curious and to explore new tasks and skills.

The following are the outcomes identified by Csikszentmihalyi in his study of *Flow*:

1. People are happier after experiencing flow because of control over their subjective experiences.

2.   People derive personal satisfaction from the activities, which are creative and challenging in the process (internal vs external satisfaction).
3.   Flow occurs during peak performance and motivates one to want to experience it again and again.
4.   The best predictor of talent was 'flow experience' - better than SAT cognitive tests, etc. Since students derive enjoyment from these flow experiences and this leads them to want to learn more, this should lead to development of enterprising learning methods.
5.   Where workers experienced flow and they stayed on the job a half hour longer (on average) each day, productivity increased. Multiply this by the number of days worked in a year and it amounts to an average of 15 extra days of contribution to the corporate growth.
6.   After experiencing flow, people report being more successful, feeling better about themselves and feeling better about living up to their own and other's expectations. (It's this recollection of flow that heightens self-esteem)
7.   Stress was reduced in people at the management level and the participants were much happier, better motivated, and felt stronger while experiencing less health problems.

As our self continues to grow, we begin to internalize worldviews that our patterning system allows us to develop into habits. These habits kick in automatically without any conscious effort. Most of our daily activities are based on those internalized unconscious actions. And so, from these daily human transactions, our worldview continues to confirm or deny what is the right thing to do. In fact, what we have just done is fallen into the trap of evolution's process of natural selection. We only adapt as much as we need to. Usually, **it takes a crisis to awaken our consciousness. Only when we become conscious again are we ready to think what we need to be doing.** For most, this wakeup call does very little except to establish one's misery and a reticence towards trying anything new and different. So in Darwin's terminology, if we fail to adapt, we are not fit enough to survive. And in our own way, we continue to sign our own death warrant.

Once we discover our inner consciousness, we can then begin to discover our meaning. By forging collaborative relationships, we embark on the task of creating our own future as we seek to achieve our vision, mission and purpose.

Our species has become too powerful to be led by instincts alone. As we become aware of the motives that shape our actions, as our place in the chain of evolution becomes clearer, we must find a meaningful and binding plan that will protect us and the rest of life from the consequence of what we have wrought.[20]

SELF-DETERMINATION

From our extensive study of entrepreneurs and enterprising people, we have been able to identify a close relationship between their activities and the concept of

self-determination. In recent years, self-determination has also become operationalized for research purposes.

Self-determination is the individual's conscious recognition that he/she can control his/her subjective reality. When people perceive that they have control over adverse events in their environment, they perform more effectively than when they believe they cannot.

Self-determined people act out of choice, based on their intrinsic needs as well as a flexible interpretation of external events. Self-determination goes beyond Maslow's hierarchy of needs. To be self-determined, one must possess the necessary skills to manage one's own environment. It is not like **'control'**, which requires a contingency between one's behaviour and the outcomes. **Self-determination is the freedom to initiate one's own behaviour along with a choice as to be in control or not.**

The complex process of initiating one's own behaviour involves a conscious analysis of one's meaning, beliefs, values, perceptions and talents, in order to identify our personal direction. In order to remain self-determined, people need to be intrinsically motivated. **Intrinsic motivation** focuses on our internal needs for achieving competence, meaning and self-determination. This intrinsic motivation helps people to energize their behaviours in order to satisfy their desires as they seek personal challenges. As these challenges require a leap into the unknown, we need to stretch our abilities and interests. Enjoyment is derived from participating in these activities, leading to increased creativity and spontaneity. By pursing self-determined goals, people achieve the productive and encouraging 'flow' that makes them want to continue.

Research by Csikszentmihalyi has also shown that self-determined people are not 'ego' driven. The difference can best be shown by describing an 'ego-driven' person to be motivated by rewards, and a 'self-determined' person to be motivated by the activity. *It is interesting to note that a common element running through the research of successful entrepreneurs identifies the 'journey', rather than the 'destination', as the key motivator.* (Timmons, Bhide)

Ryan (1982) found that when subjects were 'ego' driven, and their self-esteem depended on their doing well, they experienced pressure and tension. Self-determined people experienced an internal locus of causability. This is integral to intrinsically- (and in some cases extrinsically-) motivated behaviours. (Steers and Porter)

We interpret the world based on our memories of the past (cognitive) and expectations of the future (affective). We decide to act based on our answers to the two questions: **"Can I make a difference?" and, "Do I want to?"** The first question relies on our past experiences (cognitive), while the second relies on our intrinsic motivation (perception). Originally, these decisions are made when we are fully conscious. Once the resulting behaviours become everyday habits, they become unconscious in nature and our actions become automatic. Our mind is great at creating patterns so that it can concentrate on other things, relieved of the routine matters.

This is why humanists don't deny that we are often unconscious of what motivates our behaviour. Humans tend to restrict their experiences by repeating scripts and patterns in order to reduce anxiety, being comfortable with the tried and true. Anything that is outside this box requires effort to assess, evaluate, risk, learn, apply, create, etc.; and with all the uncertainty of what will result, it is easier to stay with the known. However, the humanists have also discovered methods that allow us to break out of these patterns of behaviour in order that we can change our view of the world. We can transcend these scripts in order to open up a higher level of human experience. **We can break our patterns to create new possibilities.**

THE WILL TO MEANING

A person's search for meaning is the primary motivation in life. This meaning is unique and specific in that it must and can only be fulfilled by the individual alone. Only then does it achieve significance, which will satisfy that person's will to meaning. As a result of the strength of these convictions, individuals are able to die for the sake of their ideals and values.

A statistical study of almost 8000 students at 48 U.S. Colleges conducted by scientists at Johns Hopkins University and sponsored by the National Institute of Mental Health found that while 16 percent of the students checked "making a lot of money"; 78 percent said their first goal was "finding a purpose and meaning to life."

The will to meaning is also supported by philosophers such as Nietzsche who states "He who has a why to live for can bear almost any how". It can be seen that good mental health involves a certain degree of tension, the tension between what one has already achieved and what one still ought to accomplish, or the gap between what one is and what one should become. Such tension is inherent in the human being and therefore, is indispensable to mental well-being. *We should not be hesitant about challenging ourselves to the point of achieving our chosen vision.* The tension is the outcome of the creative endeavours of individuals who strive to leave their present reality and thereby, create future possibilities.

If we refer back to Csikszentmihalyi's evolution of man, we see the progression from genes through culture into the self. Psychologist Viktor Frankl describes this evolution of self much in the same way.

> No instinct tells him what he has to do, and no tradition tells him what he ought to do; sometimes, he does not even know what he wishes to do. Instead, he either wishes to do what other people do (conformism) or he does what other people wish him to do (totalitarianism.) [21]

This existential vacuum manifests itself mainly in a state of boredom. Sunday neurosis is a form of depression that afflicts people who become aware of the lack of content in their lives, when the rush of the busy week is over and the resultant void manifests.

THE MEANING OF LIFE

While the meaning of life differs from person to person and from time to time, what matters is the specific meaning of a person's life at a given moment. One should not search for an abstract (general) meaning of life. *Everyone has his own specific vocation, or mission in life, to carry out a concrete assignment, which demands fulfilment.*

> Therein he cannot be replaced nor can his life be repeated. Thus everyone's task is as unique as is his specific opportunity to implement it.[22]

Logotherapy (the Psychology of Meaning) serves to make the person aware of his own responsibilities, focusing on to what or to who he understands himself to be responsible. The role played by a **logotherapist** is that of an eye specialist rather than a painter. A painter tries to convey to us a picture of the world as he sees it; an eye specialist tries to enable us to see the world as it really is. *His role consists of widening and broadening the visual field of the person so that the whole spectrum of potential meaning becomes conscious and visible to the learner.* This becomes the operating system for progress in enterprise, providing opportunities and provocations to the learner, in order to broaden their view of the world.

In declaring that each person is responsible and must actualize the potential meaning of their own life, it is important to stress that the true meaning of life is to be discovered in the world around us rather than within the person. By devoting yourself to a cause or to another person, you can actualize yourself more and, in the process, become more human. The 'flow' experience is an example of the process that produces this experience.

Thus, according to Logotherapy, we can discover the meaning of life in three different ways:

1. By creating a work or doing a deed.
2. By experiencing something or encountering someone.
3. By the attitude we take toward unavoidable suffering.

By changing your attitude, you begin to see a new meaning in life. That is why people can suffer on the condition that this suffering has meaning. However, if the cause of suffering is removed, continuing suffering could be considered a form of masochism.

Once we have gained a more meaningful understanding of our consciousness of self, we are ready to change the existing structures by creating new possibilities.

THE JOURNEY BEGINS

We have Carl Jung to thank for his insightful contributions into the fields of human behaviour and motivation. According to Jung, *our greatest urge is towards psychological wholeness and self-actualization of our inner potential*. This goes beyond Freud's notion that our view of the world and our instinctive behaviours are based simply on avoidance of pain and pleasure maximization.

In our quest to achieve our potential, we are aided by **archetypes** that are already established in our brain. As we grow psychologically, we can activate these archetypes as we continue towards self-actualization.

The first stage of growth is known as differentiation, which includes self-identification in light of cultural awareness and genetic possibilities. Asterope, in the myth of Pleiades, went through the process of differentiation by discovering her strengths and weaknesses. **By discovering a niche for ourselves, through a process of learning and assessing the external environment, we become one with the world.** We also become conscious of being conscious, giving us the opportunity to create new possibilities.

As we continue interacting with the external environment, we begin to replace previously learned sets of unconscious responses with a consciously driven method of interpreting situations in the external environment as a unique and differentiated person. This process is observed in entrepreneurs who successfully exploit opportunities and niches in the external environment.

By establishing our individual independence, we become the mythical hero in Campbell's (**reference**) mythologies (or like Asterope in the myth of Pleiades) ready to embark on a journey into the unknown. As we continue to act and interact with the vagaries of the journey, we move beyond the hero stage towards the next higher order described by Jung as the **Self-Archetype.** We move beyond learning about and mastering our environment, **actually returning to our inner-directed consciousness. This is where we exercise our whole brain - aligning figures, forms, feelings, futures and our actions, with our inner sense of meaning and intrinsic motivation of what we want to create.** This turning of our inner dreams into action is what Maslow described as self-actualization. It is at this stage that events in our lives begin to respond to our readiness to grow. It is at this stage that synchronicity, an aligning process leading to serendipity, occurs most often.

When we reach this stage, we 'lock-in' these successes as operating structures, systems, processes and strategies, going into automatic pilot. **According to Jung, we create particular lifestyle beliefs and behaviours (scripts) that we hold on to as a way of pushing anxiety out of our consciousness.** It is this new comfort zone that lulls us into a safe haven (order), protecting us from external challenges and threats to this zone.

This paradox leads to inflexibility and 'lock-in', preventing us from breaking out of these paradigm prisons in order to seize new opportunities. This holds true for entrepreneurs who exploit an opportunity, but lack the understanding that they should pass their work on to others in order to drive the enterprise to the next higher level. This is also the case with scientists who fail to network with researchers in other fields or see possibilities outside their own fields of study. Thomas Kuhn, in *The Structure of Scientific Revolutions,* pointed out that researchers often ignore information that does not fit their paradigms or worldviews. Edward de Bono, the father of lateral thinking, has pointed out that Nobel Prize winners in the sciences often came to their conclusions by discovering them outside their initial field of study. These are all manifestations of our desire to control our environment, lock in success patterns, and then seek to enjoy the comfort zone. This is the true purpose of evolution.

Our purpose, as humans, and our ability to transcend evolution's purpose requires that we constantly strive to work outside the box, seeking new possibilities. This allows us to be proactive in anticipating the future in order to identify emerging opportunities and niches. Unfortunately, most individuals and groups develop strong defences to protect their ideas and philosophical beliefs. Consistently, it is the hardened attitudes that resist rational debate and discussion about their current utility.

As humanists, Gregory Bateson and R.D. Laing have discovered that our society is characterized by irrational power struggles designed to keep control of the status quo. One of the key discoveries is what is known as the **double blind effect**, which occurs when people anticipate every idea offered by others in order to dominate the interaction. This is usually the result of parental domination in childhood, which is then perpetuated in both business and personal lives.

Every organism has a purpose. Human beings are not accidents of nature. Our social evolution includes a journey into higher levels of spiritual experience, not just for one individual but for other human beings. This is why inventions and innovations often occur at the same time in history by individuals who have no contact with one another. Our thoughts are more powerful in bringing about change than we think, and in the process, they transform existing realities into visions of a compelling future: a future which attracts others to join together on a mission that embodies a common purpose and enshrines our uniqueness and differentiation.

PERFORMANCE: THE ENTREPRENEURIAL PROCESS

Indeed, we live in a world that embodies large doses of chaos, complexity and continuous discontinuities. The certainty of the past industrial age, its reliance on predictability, incrementalism and stability has been replaced by the uncertain and the unknown. We can no longer even attempt to predict the future, let alone plan for it. The new rules of economics run counter to the economics textbooks that continue to preach lessons related to the past.

As on Mount Olympus, leaders everywhere are seeking solutions in the same old places, only to find more chaos and instability where they used to find answers. What was the best practice yesterday becomes meaningless when applied to the challenges of today in economic, social and political arenas. The challenges leaders and individuals within established organizations face are the same. Existing structures, systems, processes and strategies no longer effectively solve the challenges posed by today's emerging global environment.

Every day, new paradigms emerge to try to capture the essence of the rapidly changing business world with a comprehensive strategy. Leaders desperately latch on to these terminologies, seeking to turn their current challenges into potential opportunities. Instead, as the demand for even fresher products, services and ideas increase, they find themselves on a sinking ship without a working raft. They desperately attempt last minute heroics (trying to save the bottom line with downsizing, etc.) but, alas, the opportunity passes and the captain jumps ship to avoid the coming catastrophe.

The first step in successfully mastering this chaos is to understand and accept some universal realities in today's age of knowledge.

- A highly volatile external environment that is global in nature.
- Exponential growth of information and knowledge.
- Economic, political and societal discontinuities and dislocations everywhere.
- Escapism is demonstrated by drug and other substance use.
- Emergence of new technologies.
- Communications, computers and semi-conductors, nanotechnologies and biotechnology are the engines of the New Economy.
- The Internet is rapidly becoming a global brain, connecting everyone and everything.
- The gap between the rich and poor continues to grow.
- New environmental concerns impact on our lives and those not yet born.
- Leadership is being dispersed throughout organizations with the dissolution of traditional leadership roles.
- Bureaucracy no longer solves challenges of the present and future.
- Leadership paradigms, based on Taylor's scientific management model, no longer work.
- Underemployment exists in traditional and non-traditional sectors.

Many factors are also important in developing a paradigm for successfully existing in this environment:

- Knowledge that is linked across disciplines is most effective in solving today's challenges and discontinuities.
- The emerging science of complexity continues to link knowledge from the physical, natural, and social sciences to create effective mental models for personal and organizational growth.
- Entrepreneurs, as agents of change, create new possibilities and identify potential opportunities in the chaotic, complex and continually discontinuous marketplace.
- Small and medium enterprises are the business models of the future.
- By combining the principles of complexity science with entrepreneurial factors of success, new paradigms are beginning to emerge that will help individuals to create the needed structures, systems, processes and strategies to assist their efforts to deal effectively with the discontinuities.
- Customer/client bases and networks are constantly changing.
- The network is becoming the critical component of success everywhere.
- Creativity and innovation are at the edge of massive changes taking shape.

EFFECTIVE STRATEGIES FOR ENTERPRISE CREATION AND DEVELOPMENT: THE ENTERPRISE DIAMOND

From our research of over 2200 enterprises, we have made a number of discoveries that can assist financial executives in better understanding the nature of the entrepreneurial process.

Historically, business schools have always stressed the need for a business plan. While the business plan tends to focus the writer on key management issues, it rarely has anything to do with ascertaining the person's intrinsic motivation and his/her relationship to the business concept itself. Furthermore, the idea's potential is rarely determined by traditional market research. So what if the idea doesn't fly? What happens to all the work that went into preparing the business plan itself?

Our research has pointed to three distinct types of business start-ups: the entrepreneur, the small business owner, and the self-employed. The latter two would benefit, however, from the use of the traditional business plan. Their markets already exist and it's a matter of finding the niche to serve and becoming aware of changes taking place in the related industry.

If you are a franchisee, for example, the franchiser has the big picture, which dictates the strategy, processes and systems to be followed. Your role is to follow the system. An electrician needs to be able to identify potential users and opportunities, know the competition, and keep a good set of books in order to remain self-employed.

The case of the entrepreneur is different. Entrepreneurs are a distinct breed. At the start-up stage, they often have very few people who believe in their concept. In most cases, the financing is an act of faith in the entrepreneur's ability to get through all the challenges and roadblocks that lie in their way. This belief is usually based on the banker's perception of how intrinsically motivated the entrepreneur is. It is left to the entrepreneur to find the hidden order, which lies within the chaos we all see. This line of attack cannot be handled by the weak of heart or the traditional business plan. Some years ago, The Institute for Enterprise Education addressed this challenge by conducting a research study of the Cottage Wineries of Niagara. As part of this study, respondents were asked if they had created a business plan prior to the start-up of their enterprise. Sixty-six percent of the sample began their enterprise without a business plan. Even more significant was the fact that none of the early entrants into the wine industry had a business plan. The later entrants waited until the opportunity for the high quality wines was already identified and the market existed, before they developed business plans for their enterprises.

As a result, Leonard Pennachetti of Cave Springs Wines was able to successfully plan a new winery, a world-class restaurant and a high quality Vintners' Inn on the property of a former traditional winery that had disappeared from the scene years before. He systematically began introducing these distinct enterprises based on the initial concept of a cottage winery.

At the time of our wine study, Amar Bhide of Harvard conducted a study of *Inc 500* companies (America's fastest-growing entrepreneurial companies). His study dealt with a much more diverse group than our sample, however, the results were strikingly the same. Bhide found that 68 percent of America's fastest- growing entrepreneurial companies started their enterprises without a business plan.

So what are the alternatives?

From our review of 2200 enterprises, we have been able to observe the entrepreneurial process through four key elements of success: the person, the idea, the opportunity and the resources. As well as studying each of these four elements, we must also understand how they combine to provide the entrepreneur with a strategy to create and nurture a successful enterprise.

It is critical for bankers, financial advisors and venture capitalists to learn the constituents of each of these four elements, their interaction, and interdependence with one another. The Enterprise Diamond was designed to indicate the modus operandi of the successful entrepreneur when dealing with the external environment.

The Enterprise Diamond

The Meaning of Enterprise

The taking of initiative to achieve a self-determined goal that is part of a future vision; in order to achieve one's meaning in life, while sharing its outcomes with others in the community

THE PERSON

As individuals, entrepreneurs have a healthy, intuitive sense of self. Most have strong egos. Entrepreneurs are intrinsically motivated and create their game as a challenge to be played in the external arena. Most do not publicly announce their meaning and motivation in life, but they proudly show their vision and purpose. That is what gets them past the challenges of the day, the journey, the crisis and the chaos that arises from their interactions. It is this meaning that drives their purpose and, in turn, generates the focus, perseverance and will to take action.

Entrepreneurs have a vision in their mind, but they haven't got a clue how they will reach that ultimate destination. In most cases, they make it up as they go along this bumpy and perilous journey. Most fail in their early attempts, but their character and ethics ensure that their financiers will be with them on the next journey they undertake. The key for financiers is to establish in their own minds what motivates the entrepreneur to take this course of action in his life. How does the vision connect with the person? What individual qualities does the entrepreneur demonstrate that are consistent with successful enterprising endeavours? Some of the constituents include:

- meaning
- intrinsic motivation
- beliefs and values
- interests, strengths & talents
- focus
- drive and determination
- adaptability
- flexibility
- vision

THE IDEA

While every one of us is creative, most don't use their distinct creativity. As you have already discovered, it is easy to 'lock-in' to existing paradigms and lose sight of the possibilities around us. We are programmed to work unconsciously, so it is very rare for us to stretch our creative muscle. In most cases, we are not conscious of the possibilities we can create.

There is a difference between creativity and innovation. Creativity is a thinking process, which means that every one of us is creative. Even when you haven't used your creativity, you don't lose it. It takes your inner motivation to kick-start it. Innovation is the action side of creativity. Doing things the same way just doesn't cut it anymore. Remember the quote:

> "If you keep doing what you have always done,
> you'll keep getting what you always got."

It is when we consciously connect our unique creativity with our personal meaning, purpose, knowledge and experiences that we can begin to look at the same thing with new eyes. This requires practice - it doesn't just happen. Some elements of the idea include:

- innovation/creative
- challenges status quo
- value added
- meets conscious/unconscious needs
- well-researched and developed

When you begin to connect yourself and your idea, it becomes easier to explore the environment in order to anticipate and identify opportunities and niches. Your strong sense of self is needed to drive the idea or concept; otherwise it will die on its own. This is why successful entrepreneurs continue to persist until they find the right opportunity. It is their personal commitment that has also convinced others to join the team.

One of the best-documented entrepreneurial adventures was Mel Fisher's search for the Atocha - a ship laden with tons of gold and jewellery. It took Mel almost twenty years to find the Atocha. The only thing that kept his mission together was his vision driven by a strong sense of meaning and purpose. On many occasions, Mel could have thrown in the towel, but he and his support team persisted because they all shared in his vision. In the end, Mel discovered the Atocha and all of its jewels. He became an instant success after twenty years of uncertainty, the death of two family members, lawsuits leading to the Supreme Court and insinuations that he was a huckster. Only his personal sense of meaning and intrinsic motivation to achieve the vision, his creativity and his innovation ultimately led to the discovery of the Atocha. Thus, it is the entrepreneur's vision that becomes the force that attracts others to join in the journey. As one diver put it, "How could I miss such an opportunity, even though I would receive very little other than food and lodging?"

THE OPPORTUNITY

The debate continues. Which came first - the idea or the opportunity? It is rather like the chicken and the egg argument. Sometimes entrepreneurs identify an opportunity and sometimes they develop or discover an idea that fills a niche in the marketplace. A good illustration of this took place on a basketball court in Brazil several years ago. While refereeing in the final seconds of a basketball game with the score tied, Ron Foxcroft tried to blow his whistle to indicate a foul on the opposing team. The pea in the whistle froze and before Ron knew it, the game was over. The fans, however, were aware of what had happened. They surged onto the floor and Ron Foxcroft barely escaped with his life.

This was Ron's inspiration to create a pea-less Foxcroft whistle. It quickly became his obsession as he spent a great deal of time searching to find someone with the needed expertise to create such a device. Finally, working with an engineer, he was able to create an effective prototype. Ron's vision was clear: to create a pea-less whistle that would be the preferred choice of all major sporting events at the college and professional level. Ron's original idea emerged from a crisis opportunity; however, he still needed to convince the sports leagues that his idea was indeed a potential opportunity. After almost a decade of hard work and effort, the Fox 40 whistle became a standard at basketball arenas and football stadiums in both the amateur and professional ranks around the world. Ron also added an interesting innovation - the referee's whistle that can immediately stop the clock. This added advantage saves valuable milliseconds in the game of basketball.

Today, the Internet has become an effective vehicle that allows us to get a better grip on what is out there, what's needed, what's working and what's not. You can search the net to discover new ideas and opportunities; research your idea; access home pages of government agencies; visit some of the finest research libraries and networks and speak to others in the industry. With only a small investment, entrepreneurs can create their own web page and use it as a test for their idea's potential.

There are a number of factors involved in the identification of opportunities. These include:

- impact of global, national & regional
- economic, political & social factors
- identification of niches
- fads vs. trends
- timing

Timing is a critical factor in the exploitation of opportunities and niches. You may be the right person with a great idea, however, if the timing is not right, everything is for naught. As you can see, the first three elements have their own intrinsic factors which need to connect. Ron Foxcroft spent almost a decade getting to the point where the market would embrace the Fox 40 whistle. He had clues prior to this, but it was later that all three elements came together for him.

THE RESOURCES

If entrepreneurs are going to make an impression in the marketplace, they need to identify and gather the resources needed to support the efforts of the other three elements. Most people still think of money as the most critical resource - yet half of America's fastest-growing companies began with an initial investment of less than $10,000! Imagine. That is why the person, idea, and opportunity must connect. Otherwise, all the money in the world will not ensure the survival of the enterprise.

By far, the most critical resource is the **network**. In fact, it is the only factor that helps one to predict an entrepreneur's success. We have found in our studies that the complexity, character and quality of the entrepreneur's network and the entrepreneur's ability to effectively serve this network, determines their success in moving from a crisis situation to a 'higher order'. How effectively one meets the needs of suppliers, distributors, customers, employees, financiers, competitors and other stakeholders will determine the entrepreneur's success. The following story makes the point:

Eddie Katz, founder of Glenan Distributors, always treated traveling sales agents to coffee and a friendly atmosphere. Over the years, these sales agents knew where they could go to tell their stories. They also went to Eddie with all the deals. Eddie's business prospered and his sales to the federal government increased dramatically. In most cases, his sales price of paper to his customers was less than the price at the door of the paper company. How did Eddie explain it? Eddie pointed out that his competitive advantage and profitability was the result of buying at a low cost. By treating his suppliers as customers, Eddie was able to grow a highly successful enterprise.

Many entrepreneurs see their competition as the enemy that needs to be resisted at all costs. In our study of the cottage wineries of Niagara, we discovered that collaboration and networks among competitors created an environment of rich diversity. Each winery continued to pursue its own uniqueness, while collaborating as an industry. Today, the marketing board, government departments and support services have created a seamless network, giving the industry the impetus to embark on major growth. We are witnessing an increase in the quantity of premium wines as the industry continues to gain international stature, winning gold medals in all categories of world competition.

The spirit of collaboration is demonstrated by a myriad of examples that include: sending customers to competitors who can better meet their needs; sharing strategic information; promoting Niagara and Ontario wines, as part of advertising strategies; helping new entrants define their niches in the marketplace; sharing the expertise of the wine makers. This collaboration underlies the critical importance of developing a highly complex, high character and quality network to ensure that innovations, systemic factors and management in the industry create a whole greater than the sum of its parts.

When we look to our employees, we have a number of ways to ensure their commitment to the enterprise. One of the most effective ways is to find out what they enjoy doing. Where do they find their meaning? What is their intrinsic motivation? Just like the entrepreneur, each person must find out what really matters to him. If this approach is nurtured inside the enterprise, the commitments to helping the entrepreneur achieve his vision increases. When people are free to create alongside the entrepreneur, they present a favourable image of the enterprise to others. They convince customers and other stakeholders to want to work with their organization. One entrepreneur met every one of his employees daily. If he found anyone who had had a bad night, he sent this person home with pay. He said it wasn't altruism. This way, in his hotel business, he ensured his employees would constantly treat his customers in a courteous manner.

In a world where the new paradigm of business is to constantly innovate, develop systems, strategies and structures in order to effectively manage the four elements of Person, Idea, Opportunity and Resources; the same holds true for everyone within the enterprise. By creating an effective network inside and outside the organization, the enterprise can connect with emerging opportunities and niches in the marketplace. The challenge is to do this consistently. To understand this process, we need to study the stages of growth and development.

STAGES OF GROWTH

One of the major challenges facing small business is the management of growth. Whether we study entrepreneurs, small business owners or the self-employed, their difficulty arises during three critical interactions: innovation, technical support (quantification) and management (orchestration). Michael Gerber speaks of these three critical factors in his book, 'The E Myth'. These three critical factors occur during the three stages of the business life cycle: Foundation, Development and Maturity. This life cycle is common to all living systems. Whether we study cells, organs, societies or economies, they each follow a similar pattern of growth, development and maturity. Studies by Gerber, Adizes and Strebel all indicate similar growth processes in business.

Stages of Growth

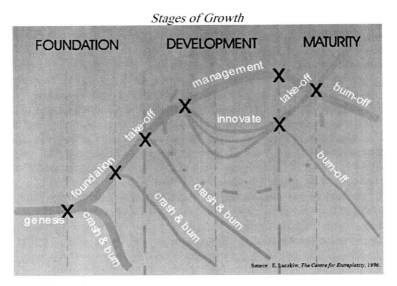

The stages of growth

In our studies of small business growth, we have discovered a pattern that distinguishes those enterprises that successfully move through various cycles of growth and those that crash and burn. While no one can accurately predict which enterprises will grow and survive and which will fail, there are specific indicators that provide us with clues.

During a study of business growth carried out at The Institute for Enterprise Education, we were able to identify seven major crisis points that a business goes through in its life cycle. When a business finds itself in crisis, its future behaviour is totally unpredictable. This is in stark contrast to the predictability people come to expect and believe in when events around them change. Within this chaos is a hidden order that successful entrepreneurs discover and exploit. However, the successful move to the next level of the growth stage is not simply the result of innovation, quantification or orchestration, but another critical factor of success: the network.

Before we go any further, let's begin with a description of each of the three stages and what needs to happen in each of these stages. This will be followed by a case study of Apple Computer, which will demonstrate what needs to be done in order to avoid the crash and burn syndrome at each of the differentiated crisis points.

Building a successful enterprise requires certain attitudes, knowledge and skills that will ensure stability during the various crisis points that occur in the life cycle of a business. This requires that the life cycle be constantly engaged in the three activities: innovation, technical patterns and processes (quantification), and management (orchestration). Together these three activities ensure that the enterprise is constantly seeking new possibilities and exploiting emerging opportunities, while managing the successful production, distribution and service to their customers. This, of course, requires a strong dose of managerial competence to ensure that the customer gets what they expect with no surprises. To build a successful enterprise, all three factors must work effectively and efficiently.

BUSINESS DEVELOPMENT ACTIVITIES: THE START-UP OR FOUNDATION STAGE

This is the riskiest stage of all and requires that a number of factors come together early to ensure that all the critical elements of the start-up are available. At this stage, the founder (entrepreneur, small business owner or self-employed) is 'one' with the enterprise; consumed by the business and working anywhere from 15 to 18 hours per day. He or she views this as a period in their life where they can change their own destiny. As a result, they remain in control of everything.

It is also a critical stage for the banker, since they may miss an opportunity to finance the next 'Microsoft'. How do you separate the successful start-ups from the thousands that will crash and burn early? That becomes a compelling question for the financier.

The enterprise needs to identify a market niche and provide evidence that it has the ability to fill the niche by delivering value to their customer beyond what is currently available. The enterprise also needs to demonstrate that the market is large enough to provide the start-up with sufficient income to grow and succeed. Thus, innovation is the most critical component in this stage, followed by the technical capability of the enterprise to deliver consistent products, service and value to the customer. The management of innovation and this technical capability become more critical as the business continues to develop the opportunity.

The New Rules of Interaction
All three factors must integrate effectively

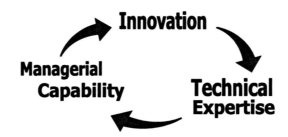

Innovation

Managerial Capability

Technical Expertise

THE DEVELOPMENT STAGE

This second stage is the result of successes experienced in the foundation stage where the business innovation was proven in the marketplace. The enterprise is facing structural and systemic challenges in the early part of this second stage. In most cases, the founder of the enterprise has successfully reached this stage because she has learned how to effectively delegate many of the roles she held in the past. While she was the innovator, technical expert and manager at the beginning of stage one, the growth of the business forced her to make a critical decision: Do I grow, stay the same or make my business much smaller?

Only a small percentage of the foundation stage enterprises will ever make it to the development stage. The major reason is that the founder has refused to let go and has been overwhelmed by the growth. Those who do succeed face a major hurdle almost immediately. While we pointed out that management is critical to this second stage, innovation is a very close second. Unless the enterprise is able to identify new opportunities that will either expand on present markets or create new products/services, it will face major challenges in the maturity stage. Most owners are lulled into a sense of false security when they see how well the system is working in producing sales and profit growth. When they wake up in the maturity stage, they notice their market share and profitability falling. However, by this time, it is too late to innovate and the business dies.

The key in this stage is not to go into the maturity stage at all. If you can effectively manage the growth of your existing product or service, while innovating new possibilities for the enterprise, then you remain in that sweet spot - a balance between the three factors. This is where successful organizations like Hewlett Packard, 3M and Magna find themselves. Sony produces over 5000 new products annually, of which ten become commercial successes. Hewlett Packard earns sixty percent of its income from products and services created in the same year. How do they do it? - By sending their innovation team to industry leaders with whom they work, hand-in-hand, to create solutions to challenges. These innovations are then sold to other businesses in the same industry. The result is that the industry, as a whole, grows, thanks to Hewlett Packard products and services.

3M inspires a culture of innovation by allowing their employees to steal an hour of time from work to work on a project of their own. If their project is accepted for development, the innovator gets to head the project management team. Thirty percent of 3M's income is derived from products developed in the past four years.

Magna spins out a new enterprise every time it reaches 200 employees. In this manner, innovation, technical factors and management continue to interact while the enterprise continues to grow.

The lesson in all of this is that the integration of the three elements (innovation, technical factors and management) is critical, while the order of their application differs from one stage to the next.

THE MATURITY STAGE

Just like the product life cycle, the maturity stage begins with a decrease in market share and profitability. It arrives suddenly without warning, as it did for Apple Computers (see Case Study). Unless the owner has identified new markets, products or processes, the business may have depended for too long on its original concept, and now new competitors have entered the field, leading to price wars and commoditization of the initial concept. As a result, the business has failed to capitalize on its initial success and must depend on price to succeed. To have any hope, the owner must literally crash and burn the existing business and begin the task of starting up all over again.

Our research of 2200 enterprises revealed a number of distinct challenges that businesses face as they move along the stages of growth curve. As mentioned, there are a number of factors, which influence the growth - or lack of growth - of enterprises. These include the three stages of growth: Foundation, Development and Maturity. Within these stages, we identified specific crisis points that uncover smaller stages. The foundation stage consists of the *genesis*, *foundation* and *take-off* mini stages. The *take-off* stage is also found in the larger development stage, along with *management*. The maturity stage shows *management* and *burn-off* as the mini stages. There are seven possible crisis points that then give rise to further movement along the curve, or crash and burn. Each of these mini stages lead the enterprise toward what we call a 'higher order'. During each of these stages, the right mix of innovation, technical factors and management capabilities must come together in the proper order, otherwise, the enterprise may flounder and die.

The key to all of this is the network of stakeholders surrounding the enterprise. A network, by our definition, consists of all individuals who are so closely affected by your actions that you need to consider them before taking the appropriate steps. The critical question is how effectively have you met the needs of your stakeholders in the network? How critical are you to their enterprise?

CASE STUDY: THE APPLE COMPUTER STORY

Apple Computer provides an excellent example of how all these stages integrate in guiding the enterprise on its journey. *Genesis* is the starting point for any new enterprise; it is the trial stage. This is the place where Steven Jobs, Steven Wozniak, and Mark Markula began to build computers for themselves. Their friends became intrigued by these personal computers and wanted Jobs and Wozniak to build them. A local parts supplier asked Jobs to build computers for him. They exchanged parts for the finished product. When orders began to increase dramatically to literally thousands of personal computers, Apple Computer moved out of the *Genesis* stage and into the *Foundation* stage. The first crisis point was whether an opportunity existed for the personal computer, which would be determined by the marketplace. As orders increased in this second mini stage, Apple faced three critical challenges: technical, management expertise and money. The second crisis stage led Apple to Wall Street where successful financing caused the price of Apple to rise threefold in a matter of months. However, the first two challenges - managerial and technical - remained. At the third crisis point,
Steven Jobs was physically removed from Apple by his board, to be replaced by John Sculley, former president of Pepsico. You may ask, what would the president of Pepsico know about computers? The answer is very little, however, he could manage growth and ensure that all systems that produced computers and dealt with markets would become finely tuned. Apple then moved to the development stage with a leader who could effectively turn chaos into a 'higher order'.

As John Sculley was turning Apple into a finely tuned business machine, he was approached by William Gates with a business proposition. If he would allow Apple computers to be cloned, as IBM had, Gates would bring his operating system exclusively to Apple and together, they would rule the computer world. Gates knew that Apple had no peer in the computer market. Sculley approached his engineers with the proposal and got a definite 'no'. After all, Apple had the standard and others would have to come to Apple to get it. Sculley was approached by Gates on at least two occasions, but to no avail. This was the fourth crisis point. It was here that Apple made the critical decision that would lead to a less than three percent share of the market.

As Sculley continued to manage Apple's demise, he was replaced at the fifth crisis point. Sales and profitability had dropped significantly and the market reacted negatively. Several other individuals took over as president. They each lasted a short period as they were replaced by a fresh face. A lot of hope was placed on Gil Amelio, the person who turned National Semi Conductor around. By this time, Apple was losing over 1.6 billion dollars with less than .3% of market share. It is here, at the sixth crisis point, that Amelio introduced new product innovations. Unfortunately, he could not interest software writers to develop programs; they could all do much better writing for Microsoft and Netscape. It was at this point, that Amelio left. He was replaced by none other than Steven Jobs - the banished son had returned. Could Steven Jobs turn Apple around? Why would Bill Gates invest money in Apple so late in the game? These were pressing questions. Was there time for Apple to re-invent itself? Were there some pieces that could help Microsoft? Why was IBM interested in Apple?

Think about the earlier discussions, related to the power of networks. Apple is still around because it has a very loyal network of stakeholders who believe, to this day, that they have superior products and programs. That might explain Bill Gates' participation. In spite of some major blunders, a strong network continues to keep Apple alive and recent fiscal quarters have been profitable for Apple.

THE ENTREPRENEURIAL METAPHOR

The challenge we set for ourselves begins with a mission to discover the meaning of entrepreneurship as an emerging force in our economy. Little did we know that the journey we would take would be full of twists, turns, challenges and opportunities, with no clear expectation of what lay ahead.

In fact, after a decade, the structures and systems that have emerged are far different from what we anticipated we would find. While we point to entrepreneurs as agents of change and creators of what has not been created before, we use them as external manifestations of those individuals who have discovered that they have a conscious mind that can transcend cultural and genetic determinants and, by the process of discovering their meaning and motivation, can help themselves to discover their true purpose in life.

ENTREPRENEURSHIP

Two critical factors are influencing today's exponential growth of entrepreneurship in our chaotic, complex and rapidly changing global economic environment:

1. An increased need for entrepreneurial talent to deal with today's emerging global reality.
2. The individual's conscious awareness of a need to discover one's meaning in a world of rapidly increasing discontinuities.

These two paths are leading people to search for new beliefs and values that lead to the creation of a vision that is compelling and comprehensive in nature, to be shared and supported by the community.

For the foreseeable future, we will continue to see an ever-increasing pace of chaos and discontinuity, leading to greater uncertainty in the economic, political and social spheres. The emerging global marketplace will continue to dictate the systems needed to deal with the complexities and vagaries of exploiting niches and opportunities that open and close in nanoseconds. *To succeed in the midst of this chaos and uncertainty will require the agility, creativity, flexibility, innovation, interdependence and vision of entrepreneurs and their enterprise units.*

By creating a compelling vision generating the needed innovation and by nurturing effective partnerships inside and outside their enterprises, entrepreneurs integrate the needed factors of success to create a larger focused force, powerful enough to exploit emerging niches, yet lateral enough to search broadly for the next opportunities.

While not everyone can become an entrepreneur in the style of a Bill Gates, Ray Kroc, Steven Jobs, Steve Stravro, Ed Mirvish, Frank Stronach, Anita Reddick or Richard Branson, *every one of us can become engaged in entrepreneurial activities that compel us to devote our conscious energies, based on our meaning and inner drive, to enlighten us to our calling in life.* If we can unite our calling with a compelling vision of a future, we will embark on a lifelong journey of complete fulfilment.

In *'The Path of the Everyday Hero,'* Lorna Catford and Michael Ray use myths to describe a hero's journey in the image of Joseph Campbell's mythologies. *By embarking upon a journey through the many challenges and land mines along the way, the leader answers the call and becomes engrossed in these challenges, leading to new discoveries, networks and celebrations. This leads to higher challenges as the non-linearity of the entrepreneurial journey continues.* This journey consists of a plethora of paradoxes that stretch your inner resources from being competitive and collaborative, creative and destructive, individual and organizational, peaceful and passionate, chaotic and orderly, and always in pursuit of an elusive vision.

In an effort to create an integrated model of an Entreplexity® organization, we began with the process of research and practice in the field of entrepreneurship and new venture creation and management. The success patterns of entrepreneurs comes under careful scrutiny, and after an exhausting review of global research, we came to several conclusions:

1. The entrepreneurial process is holistic in scope and encompasses a number of fields of study.
2. Entrepreneurs, as agents of change, create what has not been created before.
3. Successful entrepreneurs transcend their cultural and genetic determinants.
4. Successful entrepreneurs understand the need to collaborate and network within and outside their enterprise, if they are to grow their enterprise into a larger organization.
5. Entrepreneurs demonstrate a number of common traits that, in and of themselves, become a culture. These traits are common across most cultures.
6. While not everyone will become an entrepreneur, people can internalize a number of entrepreneurial habits.
7. Most people who start enterprises on their own are technicians who lack the innovative and managerial capabilities and the vision needed to drive successful enterprises.
8. Enterprise teams who demonstrate the innovative, managerial and technical expertise, while encouraging individuals to pursue their meaning, interests, strengths and talents, will grow to create new possibilities, while identifying new opportunities.

To arrive at these conclusions required a journey that took us into diverse fields of study that included such fields as anthropology, biological and physical sciences, evolutionary economics, the social sciences, as well as the emerging science of complexity. It was here that we discovered a common thread linking these disciplines that led us on to discover strategies for today's complex, discontinuous and rapidly changing global environment.

Our research into the fields of evolutionary economics, entrepreneurship, psychology and sociology identified leading-edge research into our inner consciousness, meaning and motivation. How we perceive, think, feel and act, and in what order, determines the conscious program for our decisions and actions. But asking **why** takes one towards a deeper and more meaningful understanding of our unconscious motives that determine the choices we make, both consciously and unconsciously.

As we began to pose more questions, we began to travel paths rarely used. In fact, some of the trails had barely been touched by those who went before us. It was only when we began to integrate answers, knowledge and practice from diverse sources that we began to identify consistencies that could be synthesized into an effective theory for creating change, identification of new possibilities and exploitation of emerging opportunities. We began to develop and embrace new concepts and models that started with the person and their unique inner consciousness and meaning.

We then aligned the person with an idea and identified opportunities that led to creation of a compelling vision of the future. Once this synthesis had taken place, the person began to instil an entrepreneurial paradigm into their psyche and, through practice, would develop the methodology to become an effective agent of change. Once this critical process was in place, the person could more readily begin to access the needed resources to help make the dream reality.

We were excited by the results of these discoveries, as demonstrated by participants in our learning labs. More importantly, we became convinced that we could share these experiences and knowledge with everyone who wanted to take control of their life and become an agent of change in today's exciting and highly uncertain global environment.

Our discoveries kept leading us back to the study of the entrepreneur. From our experiences, we had learned that in this particular period in our history, **a need exists to help create and nurture entrepreneurs as agents of change, at every level of our society**. In order to do so, we needed to break with the past and create a compelling vision of a future that incorporates a different set of paradigms. This is the necessary first step since it is our behaviour, within those rules and regulations that creates patterns which influence the action we take, leading to the development of new behaviours.

Our research discloses compelling evidence that people rarely change mindsets once they are developed and ingrained in their psyche. Recent research by two neurosurgeons in San Francisco, Libet and Feinstein, points out that people make decisions unconsciously. Thus, our task becomes that much more challenging when we attempt to persuade participants to begin by first consciously focusing on their inner self. *Only by changing their thinking, by reframing existing mindsets, can people again become effective participants.*

An example is the need to change when we accept a new position in a new company. Although we may rely on knowledge of the past, we begin all over again with new responsibilities and people. One of the best examples of this is found in 3M, a large global engineering-based organization. 3M has been known to select knowledge workers as leaders in organizational units, where they lack any expertise in that field. What is more exciting, however, is that these leaders are asked to rebuild existing units from the ground up. We use this example to demonstrate the effectiveness of entrepreneurial units, not only on the edge of existing structures, but also within today's organizations that have institutionalized this process.

Entrepreneurs exhibit characteristics that come from their striving instincts as genetic determinants, and it is this striving that allows them to break out of existing cultural influences and what is considered to be the conventional wisdom of the day. By creating what most consider to be the extraordinary and making it part of their passion, entrepreneurs bring about changes that transcend their thinking and experiences to create what has not been created before. The most compelling evidence shows that at the time of creation, few outsiders (or industry insiders, for that matter) see the benefit at the time of conception. Only later, once the concept has become popular, do they commence to embrace it as something they have known all along. We discovered these experiences in our research of the Niagara Cottage Wine Industry, and it has been repeated by such well-known companies as Apple, Federal Express, Hewlett Packard, Microsoft, Sony, Virgin Classics, and countless others.

In all cases, these organizations were led by entrepreneurs with compelling visions, whose mindsets demonstrated a strong sense of consciousness of self, meaning and intrinsic motivation that passionately drove the concept. Such self-determined individuals readily began to exploit niches in the marketplace, constantly innovating and creating collaborative relationships with significant partners, inside and outside the organization. Those successful entrepreneurs grew their start-ups into successful medium- and large-sized organizations. By empowering others to act entrepreneurially, new possibilities were created and opportunities exploited. New enterprises emerged from within, as well as on the edge, of these organizations (Profit 100 Study).

WHY STUDY ENTREPRENEURS?

Entrepreneurs are described as *agents of change* who break with the existing ways of doing things by creating what has not been created before.

Entrepreneurs possess a special know-how that most people on the outside cannot understand. By breaking existing patterns, regulations and rules, they literally change existing ways of doing things. They identify opportunities and exploit niches that, at first, appear as chaos, confusion and uncertainty. They rely on 'intuition' and 'judgment' to make decisions by acting upon the unknown.

As paradigm pioneers, entrepreneurs don't need to wait for all facts to come together. Fred Smith of Federal Express was strongly counselled against starting his business because conventional wisdom of the day held that the 'hub and spoke' system would not work in the package delivery system. He persisted in spite of insurmountable odds.

An entrepreneurial activity is defined as an innovative action, which either exploits an emerging opportunity or gives birth to a new product or service. Some examples of entrepreneurial activity include:

1. Product and service innovation.
2. Identification of niches.
3. Innovative ways of producing and delivering products and services.
4. Innovative means for obtaining resources to produce or deliver products and services.

Entrepreneurs demonstrate high levels of **intrinsic motivation**. People are intrinsically motivated when they seek enjoyment, interest, satisfaction of curiosity, self-expression or are personally challenged in the work they do.

WHAT DO WE MEAN BY INTRINSIC AND EXTRINSIC MOTIVATION?

Intrinsic motivation is a prerequisite to innovation. Successful entrepreneurs need to manage their own motivation, as well as motivating individuals who are part of their enterprise. Extrinsic motivation describes those individual activities that are driven by something outside of work itself, such as promised rewards or expert review. When strong extrinsic motivation is present, intrinsic motivation to carry out the task declines.

By recognizing a distinction in interrelationships and interactions between intrinsic motivation and supportive extrinsic motivation, the entrepreneur can innovate, quantify and orchestrate a growing organization.

But entrepreneurship alone is not the answer. While it serves as a metaphor for what needs to be done, it is the leadership components that ensure the success of the enterprise. While we recognize entrepreneurs for their ability to break out from the ordinary, few achieve success in growing an effective long- term organization. It is here that we separate the entrepreneur from the entrepreneurial leader.

Entrepreneurial leaders are visionaries who pursue their dreams with dogged determination and persistence. They are networkers and team builders, inside and outside the organization. They have recognized that the success of their organization depends on the complexity of the relationships they create. It is this complex web of relationships that provides entrepreneurs with a wide choice of alternatives when they face challenges that threaten the existence of their enterprise. This reduces the risks to the point where they become manageable. Only outsiders who lack an understanding of the enterprise see the efforts of these entrepreneurs as a gamble or a risk. The entrepreneurial leader has covered all the odds. She has completed her own due diligence and has avoided most of these risks.

WHAT IS AN ENTREPRENEUR?

An overview of factors that impact entrepreneurial development Because of the difficulty in defining an entrepreneur, many scholars have turned to the entrepreneurial process to provide an explanation. A number of research studies have focused on factors that shape and influence entrepreneurs including culture, family background and sociological/psychological factors. The following is a brief summary of some of their findings:

---

1) Traits Influences - A number of scientific studies have identified predominant character traits of entrepreneurs. These traits were found to influence the venture creation process and enhance its chance of success. In addition, these behavioural traits seem to motivate an individual to choose an entrepreneurial career path. Thus, according to this approach, a successful entrepreneur must exhibit the following traits:

- *high need for achievement*
- *internal locus of control*
- *tolerance of ambiguity*
- *need for independence and autonomy*
- *moderate risk-taking propensity*
- *innovation and creativity*

(Please refer to 'Entrepreneurial Traits & Motivation' for further definitions)

---

2) Cultural Influences - There are a number of areas that will argue that entrepreneurs are products of their culture. This is explained by the fact that some cultural groups see entrepreneurship as an opportunity and desirable living, while others view it as a last resort. In Canadian society, it is common to see entrepreneurs of a multitude of ethnic backgrounds and identifiable sub-cultures. In a study by the Canadian Federation of Independent Business, of the 11 nations sampled, Canada had the highest percentage of entrepreneurs who were born out of the country at 16.1%. This compares to a rate only 8% in other countries. An additional 27% of entrepreneurs in this country stated that their parents were born outside Canada and immigrated here.

---

3) External Influences - The 'push-pull' theory advocates that the motivation for new venture creation is not so much the result of personality traits, but rather the result of external factors. The existence of extremely diverse entrepreneurs suggests that personality traits in and of themselves are insufficient or inadequate to explain entrepreneurship. The explanation offered by the 'push-pull' theory is that, an individual is either **pulled** into entrepreneurship by positive environmental factors, such as a new opportunity, or **pushed** into it by negative factors, such as job dissatisfaction, discrimination, being fired or laid off. Regardless of its exact motivation, 'pull' entrepreneurship is positive and involves a relatively proactive desire to take advantage of a perceived opportunity. 'Push' factors, on the other hand, are generally negative and individuals feel they have no choice but to become self-employed. It is the general consensus that, if this latter group of individuals does not overcome this type of attitude, they are highly unlikely to adopt an entrepreneurial mindset.

4) Family/Background Influences - There is strong research evidence that entrepreneurs come from entrepreneurial families. In recent times, research suggests that 70% of entrepreneurs come from families where the father or mother is self-employed. Parents, relatives, and close friends often become role models who provide the budding entrepreneur with the aspiration to follow the same career choice. Perhaps, as a result, entrepreneurs hold a different view of the management process and business, in general, where opportunity, intention, and individualism play a larger role than for most managers. Many scholars have argued that what entrepreneurs learn, they do not learn from formal training or education, but by surviving. In fact, a formal education may not be as important in breeding an entrepreneur as it is for the individual to have been raised in an entrepreneurial environment.

5) Other Influences
a)Age - Entrepreneurs usually launch their first business between the ages of 22 and 55. However, because of the high level of energy
required to start a business, it has been found that, given the appropriate training and preparation, the earlier in life one starts an entrepreneurial
career, the better one's chances of success.
b)Work History - A large number of entrepreneurs start businesses that are usually very similar to jobs held previously, whether in small businesses or self-employed trades. As well, corporate down-sizing and increasing use of independent contractors have spurned a significant flow of talent from the large, structured entities to entrepreneurship.

Entrepreneurial Traits & Motivation
a) **High Need for Achievement** - The most frequently cited trait by researchers and practitioners is the need for achievement. This is reflected in a desire to do well in competitive situations which is seldom satisfied by the more traditional elements or career path. David McCleland in the *Achieving Society (1961)* identified three traits in his overall theory of the need for achievement. He noted that entrepreneurs: • like to solve problems and obtain satisfaction attaining goals which they have set and prioritized themselves; • take moderate risks after carefully researching options; • seek feedback either through individuals or business performance as a validation of their success and as a measure that they have achieved their objectives.
b) **Need for Independence and Autonomy** - This need is regarded as one of the strongest motivating factors underlying entrepreneurship. It represents self-reliance, and generally deals with the frustration involved in working for others. A Canadian study found that entrepreneurs wanted to start their own business because of (1) the challenge, (2) being one's own boss, and (3) the freedom to explore new ideas. Entrepreneurs tend not to rely on other people for their actions; they score low on the need for support and they favour careers where they can be their own boss.
c) **Internal Locus of Control** - Individuals who exhibit **internal** locus of control are ones who believe they control and influence their own accomplishments and failures. They seek initiative and take responsibility for their actions. On the other hand, individual who exhibit **external** locus of control believe the outcome of their actions is influenced by external factors such as other individuals, luck, chance, or fate. It has been found that internal locus of control is perhaps the one trait that is most consistently related to the entrepreneurial personality. It has also been found to distinguish entrepreneurs from corporate executives as well as successful from less successful entrepreneurs.
d) **Moderate Risk Taking Propensity** - While a few high profile entrepreneurs may project an image as high risk takers, in general, entrepreneurs have been found to be **calculated** risk takers. A moderate risk-taking propensity is typical of entrepreneurs with a high need to achieve. They also take care to research problems and consider several alternative solutions before reaching a decision. Examinations of entrepreneurs at various stages indicate that *potential* entrepreneurs may have higher risk-taking propensity when facing the probability of success or failure, but *established* entrepreneurs tend to be moderate risk-takers.
e) **Tolerance for Ambiguity** - Ambiguity in this sense is defined as a lack of complete and definitive information. Being an entrepreneur means that the person is irresistibly drawn to the unknown and to a great deal of uncertainty. They are not discouraged by an environment that requires them to make decisions based on fragments of information and a strong sense of intuition. In fact, entrepreneurs are often stimulated by this lack of certainty, and their tolerance for ambiguity allows them to perceive ambiguous situations in a positive and challenging way.

f) Innovation and Creativity - A predisposition to innovation and creativity are thought to represent a vital characteristic of the entrepreneur. One of the main distinctions between entrepreneurs and other types of managers is the former's ability to recognize and market new ideas and concepts. In addition, studies suggest a positive relationship between a high need to achieve and an innovative outlook. Whether or not entrepreneurs are really creative is debatable, as there is a strong argument that entrepreneurs simply fall into opportunities like anyone else. Perhaps the difference is that entrepreneurial individuals are able to recognize the worth and potential of these opportunities and make a living out of exploiting them.

g) Other Traits - In additional to the above, other entrepreneurial characteristics include *proactivity, intuition and vision.*

Proactivity- This trait demonstrates the ability to take control of a situation and use initiative in solving problems.

Intuition - Research shows that a large percentage of entrepreneurs rely on their intuitive behaviours in making strategic decisions. Many important decisions are based, not on fact or full information, but on the belief that an opportunity exists.

Vision - It is commonly believed that it is necessary for successful entrepreneurs to have a long-term vision. Although most develop short-term goals which they find more manageable, their long-term vision is the driving element in their success and something that most hold on to.

References: ICB "Canadian Studies" - Institute for Enterprise Education

MYTHS ABOUT ENTREPRENEURS

Myth 1*Entrepreneurs are born, not made.*
RealityWhile entrepreneurs are born with certain native intelligence, a flair for creating and energy; by themselves these talents are like unmoulded clay or an unpainted canvass. The making of an entrepreneur occurs by accumulating the relevant skills, know-how, experiences and contacts over a period of years and includes large doses of self-development. The creative capacity to envision and then pursue an opportunity is a direct descendant of at least 10 or more years of experience that lead to pattern recognition.

Myth 2*Anyone can start a business.*
RealityEntrepreneurs who recognize the difference between an idea and an opportunity and who think big enough, start businesses that have a better chance of succeeding. Luck, to the extent it is involved, requires good preparation. And the easiest part is starting up. What is hardest is surviving, sustaining, and building a venture so its founders can realize a 'harvest'. Perhaps only one in 10 to 20 new businesses that survive five years or more result in a capital gain for the founders.

Myth 3 *Entrepreneurs are gamblers.*
Reality Successful entrepreneurs take very careful, calculated risks. They try to influence the odds, often by getting others to share risk with them and by avoiding or minimizing risks if they have the choice. Often, they slice up the risk into smaller, quite digestible pieces; only then do they commit the time or resources to determine if that piece will work. They do not deliberately seek to take more risk or to take unnecessary risk, nor do they shy away from unavoidable risk.

Myth 4 *Entrepreneurs want the whole show to themselves.*
Reality Owning and running the whole show effectively puts a ceiling on growth. Solo entrepreneurs usually make a living. It is extremely difficult to grow a higher potential venture by working single-handedly. Higher-potential entrepreneurs build a team, an organization, and company. Besides, 100 percent of nothing is nothing, so, rather than taking a large piece of the pie, they work to make the pie larger.

Myth 5 *Entrepreneurs are their own bosses and are completely independent.*
Reality Entrepreneurs are far from independent and have to serve many masters and constituencies. These stakeholders include partners, investors, customers, suppliers, creditors, employees, families, and those involved in social and community obligations. Entrepreneurs, however, can make free choices of whether, when, and which they care to respond to. It is extremely difficult, and rare, to build a business beyond $1million to $ 2 million in sales single-handedly.

Myth 6 *Entrepreneurs work longer and harder than managers in big companies.*
Reality There is no evidence that all entrepreneurs work more than their corporate counterparts. Some do, some do not. Some actually report that they work less.

Myth 7 *Entrepreneurs experience a great deal of stress and pay a high price.*
Reality No doubt about it: Being an entrepreneur is stressful and demanding. But, there is no evidence that it is any more stressful than numerous other highly demanding professional roles, and entrepreneurs find their jobs more satisfying. They have a high sense of accomplishment, are healthier, and are much less likely to retire than those who work for others. Three times as many entrepreneurs as corporate managers said they plan never to retire.

Myth 8 *Starting a business is risky and often ends in failure.*
Reality Talented and experienced entrepreneurs - because they pursue attractive opportunities and are able to attract the right people and necessary financial and other resources to make the venture work - often head successful ventures. Further, businesses fail, but entrepreneurs do not. Failure is often the fire that tempers the steel of an entrepreneur's learning experience and street savvy.

Myth 9 *Money is the most important start-up ingredient.*
Reality If the other pieces and talents are there, the money will follow; but it does not follow that, if an entrepreneur has enough money, he or she will succeed. Money is one of the least important ingredients in new-venture success. Money is to the entrepreneur what the paint and brush is to the artist - an inert tool, which, in the right hands, can create marvels. Money is also a way of keeping

score, rather than just an end by itself. Entrepreneurs thrive on the thrill of the chase; and, time and again, even after he or she has made a few million dollars or more, an entrepreneur will work incessantly in a new vision to build another company.

Myth 10 *Entrepreneurs should be young and energetic.*
Reality While these qualities may help, age is no barrier. The average age of entrepreneurs starting high potential businesses is in the mid-30's, and there are numerous examples of entrepreneurs starting businesses in their 60's. What is critical is possessing the relevant know-how, experience, and contacts that greatly facilitate recognizing and pursuing an opportunity.

Myth 11 *Entrepreneurs are motivated solely by the quest for the almighty dollar.*
Reality Entrepreneurs seeking high potential ventures are more driven by building enterprises and realizing long-term capital gains than by instant gratification through high salaries and perks. A sense of personal achievement and accomplishment, feeling in control of their own destinies, and realizing their vision and dreams are also powerful motivators. Money is viewed as a tool and a way of keeping score.

Myth 12 *Entrepreneurs seek power and control over others.*
Reality Successful entrepreneurs are driven by the quest for responsibility, achievement, and results, rather than for power for its own sake. They thrive on a sense of accomplishment and of outperforming the competition, rather than a personal need for power expressed by dominating and controlling others. By virtue of their accomplishments, they may be powerful and influential, but these are more by-products of the entrepreneurial process than a driving force behind it.

Myth 13 *If an entrepreneur is talented, success will happen in a year or two.*
Reality An old maxim among venture capitalists says it all: The lemons ripen in two and a half years, but the pearls take seven or eight. Rarely is a new business established solidly in less than three or four years.

Myth 14 *Any entrepreneur with a good idea can raise venture capital.*
Reality Of the ventures of entrepreneurs with good ideas who seek out venture capital, only 1 to 3 out of 100 is funded.

Myth 15 *If an entrepreneur has enough start-up capital, success is a "sure thing".*
Reality The opposite is often true; that is, too much money at the outset often creates euphoria and a spoiled-child syndrome. The accompanying lack of discipline and impulsive spending usually leads to serious problems and to failure.

(Jeffry A. Timmons. New Venture Creation. Boston, MA: Irwin Publications, 1990, p. 20–21.)

STRUCTURING AN ENTREPRENEURIAL ORGANIZATION

The *structure* of an entrepreneurial organization became the model that we began to study as an alternative to the existing structures in both the private and public sectors. What we needed to do was to decide how this model could become an integral part of an existing organization. In 1994, we concluded the first phase of the Niagara Cottage Wine Study. Three major findings emerged from this study. They were:

1. Effective transformation of organizations and industries begins on the edge of existing structures.
2. Taking risks in creating a new enterprise enables people to take initiative in determining a future vision that liberates their individual capabilities and talents.
3. People create what has not been created before and discover new sources of opportunity by exploring in an enterprising, imaginative and interdependent manner.

While originally our research focused on the start-up entrepreneur, what we discovered was far more than we had bargained for. If this was, indeed, the way the cottage wineries transformed an existing industry, could the same be true in other industries?

A year later, we followed up the Niagara Cottage Wine Study with the 'Profit 100 Study' of Canada's fastest-growing companies. The results were encouraging. Most of these companies also began on the edge. Arcturus International became the fourth fastest-growing company within a matter of 5 years.

There are many examples that point to the entrepreneurial venture as a model for rapid growth. But, besides providing the structure, it opens up possibilities for individuals with diverse interests, strengths, talents and motivation to become part of the structure. *We believe that most bureaucratic and hierarchical structures will be replaced the entrepreneurial-structured models whose operating systems are successfully identifying opportunities and exploiting niches in the external environment.*

Research by Elizabeth Chill, Alan Gibb, Daryl Mitton, and Jeffrey Timmons has pointed out some common characteristics of entrepreneurs. Both Alan Gibb and Peter Drucker point out that these characteristics can be learned. We believe that some of these characteristics are the result of our striving instincts and are more difficult to learn. But, in the case of most teams, enough diversity exists to embody most of these characteristics. They include:

1. Self-confidence and motivation
2. Risk-taking propensity
3. Flexibility
4. Strong need to achieve
5. Strong internal locus of control
6. Perseverance and determination
7. Taking initiative and personal responsibility
8. Tolerance of ambiguity and uncertainty
9. A great deal of integrity
10. Team-building ability
11. Creativity and innovativeness
12. Vision, purpose, mission and the ability to inspire

To most individuals working in large organizations, many of these characteristics are antithetical to the structures they find themselves in. In fact, it is next to impossible to effect changes from within. The existing structure dictates against this. As noted in other discussions, most people follow the path of least resistance in these structures. The following section on Entreplexity® will take the next step into building enterprises on the edge of existing structures, still keeping the entrepreneurial mindset intact.

PROGRESS: CHANGING THE PARADIGM WITH ENTREPLEXITY®

In the heart of Scotland, in the city of Ayr, near the home of the poet Robert Burns, the next potential Microsoft is emerging. A spinoff from Digital, this latest candidate for the media's attention is another example of the New Economics of "increasing returns" mentioned above.

The partners of PRL, Bobby Parker, David Rivetts, and Jason Longo, spent their previous careers working for Digital. Parker and Rivets were the innovative engineers who created the plumbing, as they called it, for this amazing system designed to link every diverse hardware and software program into an integrated network. This system empowers users to link with other units inside and outside their organization in order to exploit new possibilities in the rapidly changing global environment. The possibilities for enhancement of global alliances make this plumbing system beneath the iceberg (as PRL describes it) of a multibillion-dollar business. So why did Digital allow this opportunity to get away?

Jason Longo, an American and former employee of Digital at its head office in the U.S., was originally sent by Digital to report on this innovation taking place in the Scottish office of Digital. Returning to the corporate boardroom, Longo enthusiastically proposed that Digital get serious about this leading-edge innovation. It had already received rave reviews from potential users of this product. Digital's reaction was typical of most hierarchical bureaucratic structures - "*It doesn't fit our core business.*" And after all our policy is "*to sell what we use, and use what we sell!*" In fact, Digital was caught in a bind. If they were to become involved, they would need to make certain it didn't compete with their existing line, and if they ignored the engineers, they could go out on their own and become competitors. In typical bureaucratic fashion, they chose to make no decision. After all, these engineers might lose interest and get serious about something more related to the organization's core business.

But Bobby Parker, the lead engineer, and Dave Rivetts, his younger protégée, decided that this project was too big to be left alone. The market had already demonstrated a strong interest and their initial sales figures were looming about $100 million a year. Longo decided to leave Digital and America in order to join the other two in Scotland and one short year later, he was calling Scotland his home. Together, in the summer of 1996, they forged a partnership and founded PRL Scotland Limited.

By embarking on their own, within the supportive incubators of Enterprise Ayrshire, the principals of PRL began their journey into the uncertain environment of information technologies.

Their first movements resembled a baby's efforts in learning how to walk; always falling and coming up again and again in vain efforts to first stand up and then to walk. Eight months later, they were moving to their new corporate offices in a highly interactive business environment. They had managed to attract the interest of some of the biggest, IBM and Microsoft, among them. They are still a long way from writing their success story but that's not the lesson from this study.

Thousands of miles away on another continent - North America - seven years prior to the start of PRL, two partners approached their superiors at one of the world's largest engineering firms, Acres International, with an innovation for cleaning environmental spills at the source. As in the case of PRL, they were handed the intellectual property and with a Visa card and basement room, embarked on a business start-up that six years later made them Canada's fourth fastest-growing entrepreneurial company according to Profit Magazine.

Further along than PRL, Arcturus Engineering, is a fascinating case study of what happens when a company goes from two employees to two hundred.

In both of these cases, as well as in hundreds of cases of emerging high growth companies, their incubation took place outside the existing organizations, and company decision makers were unable to take advantage of these opportunities not because of a lack of capital, expertise or organizational infrastructure. It happened because they were so caught up in their existing mental models that they could not understand the innovations' potential in the marketplace.

They had become 'locked in' to their existing products and services and saw these innovations as a threat rather than an opportunity. Positioned high up in a hierarchy, based on a system of command and control, these people failed to grasp the competitive advantage of these innovations. The founders of Arcturus,

Andy Panko and Tony DiFruscio, were amazed with what had landed in their laps as much as the PRL partners who were provided with state of the art equipment containing the Omega chip. The humourous part was that if they needed regular computers they would need to pay the value that had not yet been depreciated on the high-tech systems given to them.

The successful start-up of companies like PRL and Arturus exemplify that while existing structures are hard to change, there is plenty of opportunity to find niches on the edge of these organizations. Through the marriage of entrepreneurial ideals and complexity theory principles, we can show you how to successfully exploit those niches to grow new enterprises. We call this discipline Entreplexity®.

THE SCIENCE OF COMPLEXITY

Led by a new paradigm, scientists adapt new instruments and look in new places.

Thomas Kuhn, The Structure of Scientific Revolutions

Our universe is a complex system of relationships consisting of a series of structures (economic, political, and social) that interact with one another. Complexity is an emerging scientific discipline that provides us with a more meaningful understanding of the relationship between physical, natural and social systems and their interrelationships. As a science, complexity studies complex adaptive systems that include quarks, cells, embryos, brains, as well as ecologies, economies, political and social systems. These complex adaptive systems consist of diverse parts that are organically related to one another, creating a whole that is greater than the sum of its parts. All Complex Adaptive Systems (CAS) are dynamic and self-organizing in nature.

There are three key elements common to all Complex Adaptive Systems. These include:

1. **Agents** - They are known as decision-making units. (People working in an enterprise, individuals living as members of an economy, or neurons interacting with one another in the human brain.) In the Myth of Pleiades, Asterope was the agent.
2. **Rules** - Rules govern how agents make choices. (Entrepreneurs seeking to exploit niches in the marketplace) Asterope would have to deal with rules already established on Olympus.
3. **Emergent Properties** - When agents interact with one another, no one can predict what will be the final result. (Our study of 'Stages of Growth' of enterprises clearly points out the inherent difficulties in identifying which organization will move to a higher order and which will crash and burn.)

Unlike the Newtonian view of the universe where the whole could be analyzed by breaking down its component parts within the context of a stable environment, complexity is about the interaction of many agents and networks that lead to unpredictable behaviour. Simple agents, by interacting with one another, create elaborate and unpredictable behaviours. Thus, complexity, as a science, is a field that integrates knowledge across disciplines in order to give meaning to the power of the whole, within the context of a highly unstable external environment.

Complex Adaptive Systems (CAS) are different and distinct from most systems that have been studied scientifically. They demonstrate patterns of coherence under change, while taking action and anticipating futures, without central direction of any kind (self managing). A good example is how there is always plenty of food to feed a large metropolitan area without the need for centralized authority or control.

These systems demonstrate leverage where small amounts of input produce large directed changes. We can discover these points of leverage if we learn the underlying general principles that govern CAS dynamics. We are at the beginning of a journey that one day will help us solve challenges such as the current global youth unemployment problem.

Characteristics of Complex Adaptive Systems

1. They consist of a network of many agents acting in parallel. In the brain, these are nerve cells, while, in the economy, they include individuals and households.

2. Agents at one level serve as building blocks for the next higher level. These agents are constantly revising and rearranging themselves, both internally and externally, by means of competition and collaboration (co-opetition).
3. They anticipate and predict the future by use of internal models, based on individual experiences or genetic blueprints passed on from one generation to the next.
4. They are characterized by perpetual novelty. They exploit niches related to their specific needs. As they fill one niche, they open additional opportunities for others. Thus, new opportunities are constantly being exploited leading to infrastructural changes, i.e., the personal computer opportunity (Steven Jobs) and Windows (Bill Gates).

HOW COMPLEX ADAPTIVE SYSTEMS WORK

Complex Adaptive Systems (CAS) consist of many interacting agents described in terms of rules. If we are to understand the nature of interaction of these many agents, we must first be able to describe the capabilities of individual agents.

An agent's behaviour is determined by a collection of rules. These rules are based on the stimulus/response approach and are non-linear in nature. To identify the stimulus/response rules for a given agent, we must first be able to describe the stimuli the agent receives and its responses to it. Adaptation in the evolutionary sense is where the agent adapts to its environment. Experience determines what will change in the organism's structure as it makes better use of its environment. Those agents who, through experiences with the external environment, become more adept at learning and innovation will lead the field in making full use of its capabilities. Constant adaptability, flexibility and interaction with people and the environment increase the richness of experience. These increased interactions lead to greater confidence and increased motivation as demonstrated by the research of Dr. Kelly Shaver.

In CAS, a major part of the environment of any adaptive agent consists of other adaptive agents, so that a portion of any agent's efforts at adaptation is spent adapting to the other adaptive agents. An understanding of these ever-changing patterns is pivotal to understanding CAS.

Since the course of evolution is exceedingly erratic, full of false starts and temporary reversals, complexity systems meet with setbacks from time to time. This is synonymous with an entrepreneurial journey that begins with a vision of a compelling future, full of twists and turns along the way, leading either to failure or achievement. The choices one makes along the way have a tendency to grow into ever greater heights or deeper than deep lows. A number of critical choices have to be made along the way, particularly when one is confronted by forks in the road (bifurcation points) on the way to the next higher level of achievement. Each successive bifurcation point carries its own set of processes and strategies needed to move on. Failure to take the right fork will lead to a crash and burn result and prevent one from reaching a higher order. At each of these stages, new interactions lead to new possibilities and potential opportunities that are created by the agents leading towards the self-organization of the network.

What is critical to our understanding is that between these bifurcation points, we need to embody a whole new set of rules that will drive us to the next fork in the road, complete with each journey's unique set of challenges and opportunities. By employing the entrepreneurial paradigm, we begin to embody new processes and strategies.

This strategy ensures that the enterprise is in a constant state of chaos and order. To translate it in a business sense, innovation and management of growth must always work hand in hand. What is successful today will become history tomorrow so we need to constantly be seeking new possibilities in the external environment, in order to successfully exploit new niches that are constantly emerging.

The logic behind the chaos theory flies in the face of learning we received in our past and continue to see in use in the present.

Understanding complexity theory begins with a core idea. Simple objects (agents) can interact to create elaborate and unpredictable behaviour. When you participate in the process of designing a CAS and discover its effectiveness, you begin to break with the paradigms of command, control and predictability and adopt behaviours that free you to interact with the events in the environment to create these new possibilities.

Enter the computer. Model programs such as Boids can simulate systems consisting of numerous agents. If you program the model to fly in the direction of others, try to match velocity with its neighbouring boids and avoid bumping into things, an interesting journey emerges. By randomly positioning the boids in space, they soon become a flock that wheels, turns and reacts 'effectively' to objects in their path. When you add a companion to these agents, **emergent behaviour** results. The movement of the flock is not designed within each boid - it emerges when these agents interact with one another and the environment. This behaviour of the flock is discovered by means of simulation. Thus, an emergent property of a system is one that arises from the interaction of agents, rather than being engineered by agents (boids).

It is also true in the case of our own human interaction. In the same manner, an enterprise in the early stages will either succeed or fail, based on the complexity, character and quality of its networks. The same applies to success of organizations. They either grow and survive, leading to greater complexity, or crash and burn, as the Fortune 500 list demonstrates in the case of the demise of fifty percent of the participants of any number of years ago.

A compelling case study of the workings of complexity is based at the Fort Wayne, Indiana plant of General Motors. Some years ago, the plant faced a major challenge with their existing paint booths. Trucks coming off the line would be divided among a large number of paint booths according to assigned colours. Traditionally, these trucks were routed to these booths through a unit-by-unit schedule issued daily to maximize efficiency. However, when a paint booth required unscheduled maintenance or faced interruptions, vehicles would get backed up in production. An alternative approach was to throw out the schedule and turn each paint booth into an independent unit. This method would work in the following manner:

1. As the truck came off the line, it would signal its colour requirement to each booth.
2. Based on a few simple rules, the booths would bid on the work according to how efficiently each would perform the task.
3. If a booth had a colour that differed from the truck's requirements, it could not bid as efficiently. If a truck required white paint and the booth carried black, it would be less efficient than the booth that already carried white paint, due to the cost and time needed for a changeover. On the other hand, a booth with white paint was all ready to benefit from its efficiency. The most efficient booth won!

FINDINGS: (1992 - 1995)

After an initial three-year trial period at the Fort Wayne, Indiana facility, the results were dramatic, to say the least. This self-organizing paint system was unphazed by breakdowns, leading to increased efficiencies overall. The booth's colour changeovers were reduced by over fifty percent, saving over $1,000,000 a year on paint alone.

The quality of the paint jobs helped GM win a J.D. Power and Associates Award for the best fit and finish in the trucking industry. Most surprisingly, the original software consumed 10 ½ inches of paper versus 3/4 of an inch using the new approach.

ENTREPLEXITY®: A SYNTHESIS OF COMPLEXITY SCIENCES

Entrepreneurs and Jamming Jazz Bands

The results of my efforts to formulate a new science for today's changing business world have resulted in the synthesis of three distinct fields: the science of complexity, the principles of successful entrepreneurship, and the workings of the jamming jazz band.

PUTTING THE PRINCIPLES OF COMPLEXITY INTO ACTION

Our human brain is truly a jamming jazz band that makes different music in different areas of its massive physical and biochemical environment. As in the case of the jamming jazz band, the ensemble is aware of where they want to end up, but they have to rely on trust to get there. As each player improvises to the beat of his own drum, he needs to be aware of what each of the ensemble is doing as they build off one another. Ask any jazz musician and he will tell you that trust is a critical element in helping them to achieve their vision of where they end up.

THE PERSON AS A CONSCIOUS, COMPLEX AND ADAPTIVE SYSTEM

If our human brain is truly a jamming jazz band and all the evidence seems to point in this direction, then we need to take our meaning and purpose, determine what really matters and create a compelling vision.

When we embark upon the creation of a personal vision, we affect the physical, biochemical and psychological elements of the human brain. Physically, we engage what Michael Gazzaniga has identified as the interpreter in the left hemisphere. The biochemical side bathes our physical neurons by attaching to what Candace Pert has identified as the 'opiate receptor'. When we feel good about pursuing our vision, we release all the good chemicals leading to positive effects for our physical body, allowing us the needed energy to move forward past the challenges that get in our way and force us to stop and, at times, return to our comfort zones. This oscillating behaviour, described by Robert Fritz, is the result of our inability to move forward past the tension. Finally, psychologists Victor Frankl, Mihaly Csikszentmihalyi and Carl Rodgers provide strong evidence that supports the dictum that if we are truly pursuing our meaning and purpose, we lock into a state described as "*flow*". Some athletes refer to it as the "*zone*". This is where you are so engaged that you are focused on the situation (vision) and, in the process, lose all track of time and space. People in this state are not only fully engaged, but have actualized themselves to a point that only in rare circumstances will they return to the lowest rung of Abraham Maslow's hierarchy. In fact, they may even consider resorting to the tactics of hunter-gatherers and the survival of the fittest. It won't take them long, however, to get their feet on the ground and return to their journey into enterprise. This helps explain why people who are intrinsically motivated focus on the vision. They may have trouble getting there on the first attempt, but their commitment and passion will eventually get them there. Brian Tracey and others point out that successful entrepreneurs have failed an average of 2.3 times prior to achieving their vision and success.

WHAT ARE THE LESSONS WE CAN LEARN FROM THIS EXPERIENCE?

If this process works for individuals, does it also work for organizations? Of course! The challenge is to begin new enterprises (jamming jazz bands) on the edge of existing structures. This way people can begin anew. The result of these experiences is to cause each person to reflect upon their present reality and use it as a basis for going deep, while at the same time, seeking to create a personal vision that is consistent with their meaning and purpose on the one hand, and aligned with the leader, on the other.

WHAT DOES THE LEADER NEED TO DO?

While the leader needs to enunciate a compelling vision that engages every participant in the enterprise, she also needs to connect with her inner essence of being, meaning and purpose. Her role becomes helping participants to share and support the vision of the enterprise. She needs to ensure that the people, structures, systems, strategies and processes are in place to ensure that the enterprise not only consistently meets and exceeds existing customer needs, but that innovation strategies are in place to integrate learning from the customer and marketplace in order to anticipate emerging needs and niches. When everything and everyone is connected internally, the external network becomes the critical factor that not only provides the focus for the collective whole, but also creates an atmosphere of collaboration that leads to a co-evolution of the internal and external environments.

WHAT SHOULD THE ORGANIZATION'S STRUCTURE LOOK LIKE?

Structures that are mechanistic in nature create barriers to personal growth. People are expected to perform specific predetermined tasks with strict rules and regulations ensuring their compliance. This command and control type of hierarchy enforces these rules and anyone who steps outside the box does so at their own risk. Mistakes are not condoned and 'risk taking' is not part of this type of culture. Strategies embody planning techniques that once were successful in an industrial era. Today's discontinuous and highly unstable environment cannot be tied into the MBA Model of Business. In fact, as Samuelsohn points out, "we have yet to see any benefits to business brought about by over 1,000,000 MBA's".

SO WHAT IS THE ALTERNATIVE?

We have looked at the first element of complexity science agents. Our next step is to look at agent interactions with one another. What are the emergent properties of these interactions? We know that agents, especially within human communities, need to have a compelling vision of a future that they are pursuing. Otherwise, what's the point of interacting without a compelling interest?

An excellent example of how diversely different agents can interact with one another is demonstrated by the Internet. The Internet has become the medium that allows diverse agents, each following their own sets of rules, to interact with one another. There are a number of examples that demonstrate how these interactions lead to the emergence of behaviours that transcend the behaviours of any individual or small group.

Open Source Software is an example of complex adaptive systems in action. Linux software is the brain child of Linus Torwalds, a Finnish programmer now residing in the United States. Torwalds made his secret code available to everyone on the web. The inspiration for Linux came after Linus could not afford to buy a commercial version of Linux-the operating system popular in academic and business areas. The strength of Linux lies in the field of software development known as 'open source'- the DNA of computer programming. It is freely released to anyone who wants to see it and bring about modifications. It is like having the secret formula revealed to you. Just think if Bill Gates would make Microsoft's code freely available to everyone? What a treat to those programmers out there seeking the challenge. What if 'Coke' were to reveal its secret to all? What would the new 'Coke' look and taste like?

Think of the pharmaceutical field. What if one of the giants in the field would reveal their latest cancer diagnostic system? What if they revealed some recent discoveries in preparation? Think of the multitude of ideas, theories and concepts that would be provided to scientists in the firm. This collective consciousness from around the globe would ensure the growth of the open source pharmaceutical companies.

The Human Genome Project is but an early attempt to link the physical, natural and computer sciences in deciphering the genetic code. If we truly want to extend the benefits of knowing the code towards the elimination of disease, we can put this method into action. By harnessing the collective wisdom of developers worldwide, Linux has been able to gain a peer review of how the best innovations are adapted, resulting in rapid solutions to life's pressing challenges. Otherwise, what's the point of constantly reinventing the wheel or working on the same challenges in thirty diverse locations? By pooling the talent, exponential returns will greet all participants. It is truly this type of interaction that allows agents interacting with other agents, each following their sets of rules, to achieve a higher order. In the end, the community and society, as a whole, benefit.

THE JAMMING JAZZ BAND: A METAPHOR FOR CREATING ORGANIZATIONS WITH A CONSCIOUSNESS

Each of us is a living system participating within a chaotic, complex and rapidly changing global environment. As living systems, human beings demonstrate a genetic propensity to self-organize. Because human behaviour has been steeped in the traditions of the industrial era, we are prevented from returning to our natural roots so that we cannot effectively adapt to this changing environment. However, we can break out of evolution's grip in order to rewrite both our cultural and genetic plan. First, we need to become conscious - conscious of who we are and why, and what needs to be done, in order to break the chains of our past mental models and discover the essence of our being. As we begin to 'self-organize', we develop a shared understanding of what is truly important and behaviourally acceptable. We arrive at the realization that we, indeed, have the capacity to make a difference and a compelling interest to do so. It is how we put it into action that will lead to superior performance.

A jamming jazz band is a metaphor for how effective organizations should work. Each performer pursues his 'self-determined' distinctiveness, while sharing a vision based on the group's creative endeavours. By sharing their individual experiences with others, each performer pursues his own purpose as part of a mission to create music by means of improvisation. As a result, each performer self organizes as he performs.

This highly interactive process relies on the following twelve pre-requisites:

1. High degree of competence
2. Strong sense of trust
3. Constant awareness of each other's uniqueness and differentiation
4. Diversity of talents
5. Constant communication and interaction
6. Adaptability and flexibility
7. Strong sense of intrinsic meaning and motivation
8. A compelling vision of achievement
9. Management by self-organization
10. Changing nature of leadership, based on needs
11. Sense of humour
12. Improvisation

By emphasizing a strong sense of individuality, combined with diversity of talent, each performer in the network is free to pursue her uniqueness as a musical piece emerges that is far more powerful than the sum of its parts.

Whether our focus is on jazz musicians or participants within an organizational context, success is based on the effective integration of the twelve factors above, leading to ever-increasing complexity and higher achievement. This process occurs naturally and spontaneously, without the benefit of a command/control hierarchy. The organization of a jazz band represents the workings of all living systems.

When we look at most organizations, however, we discover leaders who treat participants as machine parts reduced to performing planned tasks in order to gain extrinsic rewards. By imposing control from the top down, efforts at the ground level are suppressed, leading to losses of customer niches and opportunities. When leaders view people in this mechanistic fashion, they fail to consider their distinct talents which need to be free, in order to allow them to make a maximum contribution to the organization's future.

Only by nurturing everyone to discover their individual sense of meaning, will people become conscious of who they really are and what they need to be doing. When we discover our inner sense of meaning, we direct our attention to what really matters to us and what we need to be doing. When we are intrinsically motivated, we develop the needed energy to create our future, by attracting people and events in the external environment to shape our vision. Not only do we find enough energy to persevere, but we also develop the needed passion that inspires ourselves and others.

All living systems are in a constant state of change. In the case of the jazz band, musicians begin with a vision of the end result without a master plan; however, they are always tinkering with and attempting new variations. At times, they even bring in audiences as participants in their performances, thus leading to further improvisation. By working the edges, a higher musical order emerges.

Does this mean that the musicians are acting irresponsibly in attempting these new approaches? Absolutely not! Amid this chaos, they are clear about their purpose and their own set of values and what they stand for. It's the consequence of these distinct and deliberate actions that leads to the system's synchronicity.

Organizations can learn a great deal from the concept of the jazz band. Once they begin to reflect on who they are and what they believe in, they then need to ensure that every participant is free to create and contribute in her own differentiated way towards the achievement of the organization's goals. At times, participants will find themselves in the midst of chaos and disorder and mistakes will no doubt be made, but the learning that results will more than make up for these slippages.

Every organization must continually evaluate whether or not it is providing a nurturing environment for its participants. If the organization lives according to its core beliefs and values, then the whole will become greater than the sum of its parts. When we compare leadership in a jazz band and leadership in a symphony orchestra, the distinction is clear: In the former, leaders are not visible in the midst of chaos, complexity and improvisation. In the latter, the conductor is highly visible and controlling in his efforts to achieve the creator's vision. In today's discontinuous environment, the jazz band serves as a highly effective metaphor for dealing with these external challenges.

THEORY INTO PRACTICE EXERCISE: STRATEGIES FOR CREATING ENTERPRISES ON THE EDGE

"All Things Are Difficult Before They Are Easy."
- John Morley

In order to champion a vision, people must be willing to deviate from conventional methods and strive, through seemingly endless hurdles and roadblocks, as they confidently, with a great deal of courage, move towards achievement of their goal. First and foremost, people need to accept the fact that they have the capability and capacity to change their present reality. Before attempting to create a vision of the future, emphasis must be placed on the individual. People need to first return to their roots, the consciousness of self, in order to discover their true meaning in life and their essence of being. Only when we are truly in tune with our inner self, can we hope to become effective participants within the larger organizational context.

Michael Ray (1989) points out in 'New Traditions In Business' that "the gateway from the old paradigm to the new is the individual, and changes in the individual come from the inside; from inner consciousness or spirit. People involved in business transformation have come to it from their own personal transformation."

We have learned that developing a compelling vision of a future will integrate the **talents** of each participant with the emerging **cultural domain**. This cultural domain consists of all differentiated participants integrated within a system of rules that defines ranges of performance. When the talents and the cultural domain are integrated with the **external field**, consisting of individuals and organizations whose task it is to determine the value of performance, a synergistic order emerges, leading to the vision's successful outcome.

When people align their inner self with others, both inside and outside their organizational structures, their internal energy is focused on the challenge, leading to an increase in confidence and intrinsic motivation. By creating the kind of work that is an extension of their being, people create new possibilities and identify opportunities that bridge the gap between the current reality and the future vision. As part of this series of interactions, we begin to recognize the advantage of taking risks, making mistakes, and learning from these experiences. As we build trust with others, based on their differences, this differentiation and integration leads to greater personal empowerment, as well as towards a higher level of evolution known as complexity.

In an analysis of responses from about 400 managers at a Fortune 500 Company, Gretchen Spreitzer (1995-96) was able to identify empirically four dimensions:

1. **A sense of meaning.** Work was important to the participants.
2. **A sense of competence.** They were confident about their capabilities to perform.
3. **A sense of self-determination.** They felt free to choose how they did the work.
4. **A sense of impact.** They felt they had influence in their units.

Spreitzer also found that empowered people saw themselves as more innovative than less-empowered individuals. Both subordinates and superiors also gave empowered people significantly higher scores on measures of innovation.

From this study, Spreitzer demonstrated that empowerment is, indeed, worth the effort. Spreitzer also identified four organizational conditions that lead to an empowering environment:

1. **A clear vision and challenge.** (They know where the organization is going.)
2. **Openness and teamwork.** (A sense of participation, openness, flexibility, creativity and teamwork.)
3. **Discipline and control.** (Goals, tasks and lines of authority are clearly defined.)
4. **Support and a sense of security.** (Support is provided by subordinates, peers, superiors and others.)

Personal Empowerment Questions:

1. How can I increase my own sense of meaning and task alignment?

2. How can I increase my own sense of impact, influence, and power?
3. How can I increase my own sense of competence and confidence to execute?
4. How can I increase my own sense of self-determination and choice?

By considering these questions and discovering answers inside ourselves, we can truly make a genuine contribution by shifting responsibility from others to ourselves.

CREATING A COMPELLING VISION OF THE FUTURE

The term *vision* has become one of the most overused and least understood concepts in the field of organizational transformation. While there are a number of operational definitions, we have chosen the Collins-Porras (1991) vision framework developed at Stanford University, as both measurable and pragmatic. Collins and Porras identified three major components that make up the vision framework. These include:

1. **Core beliefs and values** are the fundamental motivating principles that permeate the organization. They are the extension of each person's beliefs and values.
2. **Purpose** is derived from these core beliefs of the organization. It serves as the reason for being. It is something that is worked towards, but is never achieved.
3. **Mission** is the focal point, the major goal that people strive to achieve. An example often used is the moon mission. John F. Kennedy, President of the United States, stated, "This nation should dedicate itself to achieving the goal, before this decade is out, of landing a man on the moon and returning him safely to earth."

The creative process is the bridge between the present reality and a compelling vision. It is the driving force that affords the opportunity to get out of the box to create what has not been created before. It mirrors actions of entrepreneurs within the external environment. By breaking out of existing patterns of perceptions, people direct attention at new situations, thereby exploring outside the proverbial box. The mission becomes the force that drives the creative process. The creative process ensures that the needs of the organization and its stakeholders are met.

Tension is created as a result of these actions and interactions. It is the result of all discrepancies faced by individuals interacting with one another, both inside and outside the structure, in their attempt to move from the present reality to that of the future state. When all the elements come together, the mission has been completed. Individuals are now ready to face the next challenges as they seek to embark on another mission.

To be effective, the creative process needs to embody a holistic approach that begins with each person and their internal motivation to create a future vision. This vision needs to be aligned with an inner sense of meaning (personal purpose) and determination. The creative process differs in both the outcomes it produces and the journey travelled. It all depends upon the creator and her or his interactions with the external environment. The key is to continually focus on the vision. You cannot predict how you will arrive at the vision for there will be many roads that will get you to it. There will be times when you will get lost along the way; there also will be times when you discover new possibilities along the edges that may lead you along undiscovered paths. And, sometimes, in the middle of the forest, you will begin anew that relentless pursuit to achieve your vision.

Robert Frost's, *The Road Not Taken,* sums up his experience in the final paragraph when he writes:

> I shall be telling this with a sigh
> Somewhere ages and ages hence
> Two roads diverged in a wood, and I –
> I took the one less travelled by,
> And that has made all the difference.

The creative process, the defeat of habit by originality, provides each one of us with an opportunity to change our present reality on the road to achieving a compelling vision of the future.

This vision incorporates our **beliefs and values, our purpose and our mission** in life. While our core beliefs and values measure the rightness of the vision; our purpose is based on what matters to us and our meaning; and the mission answers how we will work towards the achievement of the vision: The more meaningful the vision, the greater the chance of its achievement. These three factors embody the essence of what make a vision not only achievable but sustainable over the long run.

CORE BELIEFS AND VALUES

In creating a vision for your organization, you need to begin by focusing on your individual beliefs and values as the building blocks of your personal vision. These core beliefs and values form the essence of your decisions and actions evolving into a guiding philosophy for your organization.

Your beliefs and values form the fundamental motivating principles and tenants about what is important in your life, how you should act, your paradigm of human beings, your role in society, your distinct world view and all those other things you will not compromise.

These core beliefs and values are analogous to your body's genetic code, always ready to shape your role. As they belong to you, you project them and have an impact on people with whom you interact.

Some examples of core beliefs and values found in organizations include the following:

- We intend to make a contribution to society through our products, services and the way we deliver them.
- We believe that we should be, for all involved, a place of realized potential.

– We believe in doing a really outstanding job - we simply don't want to do anything without high quality.
– We believe in personal growth, both for ourselves, as individuals, and over the long term of the organization.
– We are committed to the highest standards of ethics and integrity.
– We are committed to research that matches science to the needs of humanity.
– Do unto others, as you would have them do unto you!

PERSONAL BELIEFS AND VALUES

Values form the basis of every human endeavour.

– **Values are distinct**. They go to the root of your uniqueness and differentiation.
– **Values are enduring**. Values pass the test of time. They become the thread that weaves through your whole person.
– **Values are influential.** Values capture the spirit of who you really are.

As an individual or, for that matter, as a member of an organization, what values do you think should consistently be seen in every personal attribute and organizational culture? (See list of Common Personal Values which follows.)

COMMON PERSONAL VALUES

Accomplishment, Success	Friendship	Privacy
Accountability	Fun	Progress
Accuracy	Generosity	Prosperity, Wealth
Adventure	Gentleness	Punctuality
All for one & one for all	Global view	Quality of work
Beauty	Goodwill	Regularity
Calm, quietude, peace	Goodness	Reliability
Challenge	Gratitude	Resourcefulness
Change	Hard work	Respect for others
Charity	Happiness	Responsiveness
Cleanliness, orderliness	Harmony	Results-oriented
Collaboration	Health	Rule of Law
Commitment	Honour	Safety
Communication	Human-centered	Satisfying others
Community	Improvement	Security
Competence	Independence	Self-givingness
Competition	Individuality	Self-reliance
Concern for others	Inner peace, calm, quietude	Self-thinking
Connection	Innovation	Sensitivity
Content over form	Integrity	Service
Continuous improvement	Intelligence	(to others, society)
Cooperation	Intensity	Simplicity
Coordination	Justice	Skill

Creativity
Customer satisfaction
Decisiveness
Determination
Delight of being, joy
Democracy
Discipline
Discovery
Diversity
Dynamism
Ease of Use
Efficiency
Enjoyment
Equality
Excellence
Fairness
Faith
Faithfulness
Family
Family feeling
Flair
Freedom, Liberty

Kindness
Knowledge
Leadership
Love, Romance
Loyalty
Maximum utilization
 (of time, resources)
Meaning
Merit
Money
Oneness
Openness
Other's point of view, inputs
Patriotism
Peace, Non-violence
Perfection
Personal Growth
Perseverance
Pleasure
Power
Practicality
Preservation

Solving Problems
Speed
Spirit, Spirituality in life
Stability
Standardization
Status
Strength
Succeed; A will to -
Success, Achievement
Systemization
Teamwork
Timeliness
Tolerance
Tradition
Tranquility
Trust
Truth
Unity
Variety
Well-being
Wisdom

(Retrieved from:
http://www.gurusoftware.com/GuruNet/Personal/Topics/Values.htm)

Exercises and Applications

In this section, the exercises and applications Gene used in various parts of the Enterprise Education Curriculum are presented as learners received them. The reader will note that the exercises are of such character that they are adaptable to other circumstances.

The first exercise involves the articulation of personal beliefs and values, followed by a group synthesis of commonly held (or negotiated) values. The development of organizational purpose, mission and vision follows with examples drawn from corporate and other contexts.

PERSONAL BELIEFS AND VALUES EXERCISE

Prior to the development of organizational purpose, vision and mission, it is critical to establish a common set of values for the team.

First, in this exercise, team members are asked to each select their top five personal beliefs and values, and then rank order them from one to five, five being the most important (Refer to Common Personal Values in Personal Beliefs and Values Section.) Once this part of the exercise has been completed, team members will be asked to agree on a common set of values. Later, the team will be asked to select the final five.

The key issue you need to pursue is: What beliefs and values do you feel should be manifested consistently in every personal and organizational aspect?

PURPOSE

Purpose is an outgrowth of your core beliefs and values. It is the reason for your existence - your raison d'être. Your sense of purpose phases in with other people who are part of the enterprise. A key element of purpose is that you always work toward it, but you never quite reach it. It is like following a guiding star at a distance, but no matter how many mountains and valleys you cross, you can never reach it.

People with a purpose in their lives will never be at a loss to find meaningful work. As Viktor Frankl points out in 'Man's Search for Meaning', "He who has a *why* to live for, can bear almost any *how*."

It has been demonstrated on a number of occasions that good mental health involves a certain degree of tension, the tension between what one has already achieved and what one still aspires to achieve. Such a gap usually exists in most of our lives. Understand that tension is inherent in human beings and that it is necessary if we are to grow. We should not be hesitant about challenging ourselves to the point of achieving our vision.

THE ORGANIZATIONAL PURPOSE

Every organization has a purpose. Most have never formally articulated it, however. To begin with, leaders need to think through the question, "What exactly is our purpose?" Keeping your answer to one sentence helps you to clarify what your organization is all about. Once you have a clear understanding, you will need to test your actions to determine if they are consistent with your purpose. Some of the examples of purpose that follow this section were collected by Collins and Porras, and can apply to both public and private sector organizations. The reason is that purpose is a motivating factor and not a differentiating one. Thus, it is possible for two distinct organizations to have a similar purpose. It is the **mission** that distinguishes one from another.

A statement of purpose should convey the reason for your organization's existence; how it fills human needs and creates an impact on the world. A good purpose statement is broad, fundamental, inspiring and enduring. It should guide the enterprise for a hundred years.

Examples of Purpose:

Giro exists to make people's lives better through innovative, high quality products.
Giro Sports Design

To help leading corporations and government be more successful.
McKinsey & Company

To be a company that gives unlimited opportunity to women.
Mary Kay Cosmetics

To improve the quality of human life through innovative human therapeutics.
Celtrix

To make the world more secure.
Schlage Lock Co.

Our purpose is to provide solutions that protect the environment and improve the quality of life.
Kennedy-Jenks

HOW CAN YOU DISCOVER YOUR ORGANIZATION'S PURPOSE?

Collins and Porras recommend a five stage "*why*" process that will help focus on your organization's purpose. Try to tie your product or service to a more fundamental need.

Let us use one of the previous examples provided by Celtrix.

> *"To improve the quality of human life through innovative human therapeutics."*

Now, let's create some *why* questions to go along with it.

1)   *Why* do we want to do this?
2)   *Why* is this important?
3)   *Why* do we want to dedicate a portion of our lives to this?
4)   *Why* should we continue to exist?
5)   *Why* would the world lose if we ceased to exist?

Another method would begin with the following statement.

> *We make (provide)* _____ *product (or service).*

Then, ask "*why*" five times. After five "*whys*", you will find yourself getting down to the fundamental purpose of the business.

Example:

> *"We make outdoor clothing."*
Why?
> *"Because it's what we know best and what we like to do."*

Why is that important?
> *"Because it's the best way to make innovative, high quality products that people will pay well for."*

Why is that important?
> *"Because that is how we can continue to be financially successful."*

Why is that important?

> *"Because we need the credibility of being a successful business and the resources to do business in the way we think it ought to be done."*

Why is that important?

> *"Because we ultimately exist to be a role model and tool for social change, and the only way we can do that is to be financially viable and successful enough to have the rest of the business community looking at us as the role model."*

Having selected the purpose for your enterprise, you are now ready to differentiate yourself by focusing on the mission.

MISSION

Your mission statement will answer the question '*how*'. It is the action side of the visioning process.

Unlike *purpose*, a *mission* is achievable. It takes your values and beliefs, along with purpose, and translates it into an energizing, highly focused goal. It should be crisp, clear, bold and exhilarating. Once you complete your mission, you return to purpose in order to set a new mission.

As an analogy, your purpose is the guiding star always out there on the horizon, but never quite attainable, but pulling you forward. Your mission is the mountain. Once you reach the summit, you sight the star and turn to climb another mountain.

A good mission entails risk, a bit on the unreasonable side, but intuitively possible. It definitely has a finish line and a specific time frame for achievement. John Kennedy created the moon mission.

> *This nation should dedicate itself to achieving the goal before this decade is out, of landing a man on the moon and returning him safely to earth.*

Most corporate mission statements are different from the models recommended in this exercise. They are **who cares?** statements and are totally ineffective in inspiring a team effort.

A poor example of a typical corporate mission statement:

> We provide our customers with retail banking, real estate, finance, and corporate banking products, which will meet their credit, investment, security and liquidity needs.

Can you think of other such statements that you have seen in the past?

Missions are generally from three to twenty years in length. The key is ensuring that once it is fulfilled, you are ready to move on to a new one.

HOW TO CREATE A MISSION STATEMENT THAT WORKS

1. Your mission must have a passion.
    We're going to make _____ the pre-eminent manufacturer in the

    _____ field within
    10 years.

2. There are risks involved.
    When you set a mission, you depend on the intuition to carry the day. You
    can never prove that your mission is 100 percent achievable. But once you
    make a commitment to the challenge, the probabilities of success change.

    Think of our mountain example. If someone would put you on the mountain
    and close the escape route, your probability of success would be greater
    than if you could always choose the escape route. Why? Because you
    would be more committed.

3. You must be sincere in describing your mission. You must want it badly
    enough to make personal sacrifices in order to attain it. Experience shows
    that a great mission lacking honesty never works and becomes counter
    productive. When people learn about the lack of sincerity, they lose respect
    for the business and the people at the top.

FOUR TYPES OF MISSION

1. Targeting
2. Common Enemy
3. Role Model
4. Internal transformation

1. **Targeting** - set a clear target and aim for it. The Kennedy moon project is a
    good example of this. Another approach used in targeting is to set a goal of
    taking the enterprise to a new level of dominance or industry penetration. If
    you use money as a quantitative measurement, you may need to excite
    people by tying in to something that is meaningful for them. This means
    such things as job security and growth.

2. **Common Enemy** - picking a common enemy and seeking to destroy it,
    especially if you are the underdog, is a great motivator to instilling unity of
    purpose. Pepsi's mission to beat Coke is a classic example. An extremely
    powerful common enemy mission is when an organization has its back
    against the wall and it identifies a common enemy. The shortcomings of
    this type of mission are that once you have defeated the enemy, there is
    nothing left to motivate.

3. *Role Model* - using organizations that you identify as role models is excellent for small business start-ups. *To become the IBM of the financial industry,* is an example. *To be the Rolls Royce of the paper products industry,* is another.

4. *Internal Transformation* - this mission is rare and is usually reserved for those existing organizations that require dramatic restructuring. An example from General Electric

> *We are committed to developing the sensitivity, the leanness, the simplicity and the agility of a small company.*

PUTTING IT TOGETHER

Now that you have explored the three components of your vision, you are ready to prepare your final draft. Here are your guidelines in summary form.

1.	Core Values and Beliefs	Change seldom, if ever
2.	Purpose	Should last at least 100 years
3.	Mission	When you complete one mission, you can begin to start another (3 - 20 years)
4.	Strategy	Revise annually and redo for each new mission
5.	Tactics	Always flexible in order to adjust to changing conditions.

PREPARING THE VISION

In preparing your vision, it is essential that it is clearly understood and shared by key people in the organization. Whether it comes from the top or the grass roots, the important fact is that it is clear and shared by all participants who are committed to its pursuit.

Remember that you need not be a charismatic person with a vision. The task is to build an organization with vision. People come and leave; great organizations can be around for centuries.

THE VISIONING PROCESS

When we seek to create a compelling vision of a future, we need to consider each participant's beliefs and values as building blocks for the core beliefs and values of the enterprise. By demonstrating a healthy respect for each person (trust) and by proclaiming a commitment toward a common purpose, we form the foundation for the creation of a compelling vision of the future. The mission aspires to fulfil the vision, as well as helping each participant to achieve her or his personal goals. This self-actualizing process ensures that a common focus always remains in spite of day-to-day challenges that tend to sideline the original vision.

But, an equal emphasis should be placed on external stakeholder such as customers, suppliers, distributors, financiers and competitors. By integrating their needs with the purpose of your organization, everyone becomes involved in helping each other to achieve their mission.

If it is to survive in today's chaotic, complex and rapidly changing global environment, the enterprise must commit to not only providing the highest quality customer service once they have identified a niche, but it must also commit to working with the customer in a relationship that puts them side-by-side, in attempting creative solutions to the many challenges they face daily. Hewlett Packard derives sixty percent of its income from products and services it developed in the same year. They do so by working with customers at the customer's place of business. The products they create can then be sold to other organizations facing similar challenges.

Engineering a Vision

Several critical factors contribute towards creation of a compelling vision of a future. These include:

1. A vision must be positive and inspiring.
2. To create a compelling vision, every participant must stretch outside her or his boundaries to create what has not been created before.
3. The vision must be worth the effort.
4. The vision needs to be comprehensive and detailed.
5. Each participant must see their contribution as meaningful, based on their individuality and involvement.
6. When everyone agrees on the direction of the vision, energy must be focused on its achievement.
7. When positive energy is concentrated, a convergence of these distinct forces opens up new niches and opportunities.

FACTORS THAT CONTRIBUTE TO ACHIEVEMENT OF A COMPELLING VISION

In order to achieve the vision, the following factors need to be considered in its creation:

1. Understanding the customer's present and future needs.
2. Innovation must be the nurturer of value-added services and systems that provide the customer needs.

3. Intrinsically motivated people, whose core beliefs and values are consistent with the organization's purpose, ensure growth of the enterprise.
4. The utilization of the most effective and efficient policies, processes, practices and programs designed to deliver outstanding leading-edge performance.
5. Responsiveness to the customer's immediate needs ensures successful development of new products and services.
6. Reliability based on consistent supply or services over the long term.
7. The result of these actions includes:
8. Vision drives industry leadership.
9. Innovation provides customers with the highest value.
10. Intrinsically motivated people provide sustained creativity and high productivity.
11. Competitiveness is assured by a combination of effectiveness and efficiency.
12. Responsiveness leads to virtual short-term solutions.
13. Reliability provides the needed comfort zone for customers seeking long-term relationships.

Most leaders, managers and participants are aware of what needs to be done in order to succeed as an enterprise. Most, however, fail to focus on each person's contribution to the achievement of the vision. Thus, it becomes critical that each participant integrates his own beliefs and values with the core beliefs, values and purpose of the organization. Only by becoming a force of one will the enterprise be able to survive the day-to-day challenges, while maintaining the needed focus on the compelling vision of the future.

As the Old Testament states: "Without a vision, people perish." In today's global environment, this statement takes on greater meaning. People create the structures, systems, processes and strategies that transform existing realities. People need to always be in a position to shape and reshape these forces. Only then, will each individual's contribution provide the meaning that gives greater impetus to their being. Together, each person will share in helping one another shape a compelling vision of the future.

CREATING YOUR FUTURE: THE ENTERPRISE DIAMOND EXERCISE

The purpose of this exercise is to empower all members of the team to create an enterprise of your very own. In order to consider all factors that are essential towards formulation of a compelling vision, we have prepared this step-by-step strategic process to ensure that you cover all the relevant areas of consideration.

This should not only become an exciting experience as you participate in this very creative process, but it can also be very fulfilling, particularly, when you are afforded an opportunity to work to your interests, strengths and talents.

The creation of a compelling vision of the future begins with an exploration of the purpose, which is based on the core beliefs and values of the team. The mission answers the how question, which leads us to identification of goals and objectives, indicating how you are going to get there.

First, you will begin with an actual exploration process that will align and synchronize elements of success: person, idea, opportunity and resources. This draft presentation will be the focus of this feasibility experience which will lead to a future challenge, where you will move from the present reality towards actually developing the Entreplexity® discipline into a highly efficient and empowering experience.

Introduction

Briefly describe the services you will be offering through your emerging entrepreneurial unit.

_____
_____
_____
_____
_____

Person (People)

1. What is the compelling interest of your people for creating an entrepreneurial unit?

    _____
    _____
    _____
    _____
    _____
    _____
    _____

2. What personal factors will contribute towards the success of this enterprise? (attitudes, knowledge, skills)

    _____
    _____
    _____
    _____
    _____
    _____
    _____
    _____

3. What specific human needs of your unit's participants will this experience satisfy?

    _____
    _____
    _____
    _____
    _____
    _____
    _____
    _____

4. What additional external or internal factors will influence the shaping of the people strategy?

    _____
    _____
    _____
    _____

Idea

(a) Illustrate and explain the mechanics of your service enterprise and what it is designed to do.

    _____
    _____
    _____
    _____
    _____
    _____
    _____
    _____

(b) How do you differentiate this idea from what is currently taking place?

    _____
    _____
    _____
    _____
    _____
    _____
    _____
    _____

(c)   What consumer need does it answer?

_____

_____

_____

_____

_____

_____

_____

_____

(d)   What do you see as your idea's strategic advantage?

_____

_____

_____

_____

_____

_____

What laws, regulations and policies apply to your idea?
(Indicate how you can operate in this manner based on
current structures, systems, processes and strategies in
place.)

_____

_____

_____

_____

_____

_____

_____

(b)   Have you determined what you need to do to fulfill
        these requirements?

_____

_____

_____

_____

_____

_____

_____

Discuss any environmental factors that may impact on your idea.

_____
_____
_____
_____
_____
_____
_____

(b)   Include some 'wild card' possibilities that may surprise you.

_____
_____
_____
_____
_____
_____
_____

4.   How does your idea affect the general welfare of society?

_____
_____
_____
_____
_____

5.   Why do you think that you can successfully launch this business idea?

_____
_____
_____
_____
_____

6.   What additional research must you do in order to shape this concept before you begin its implementation?

_____
_____
_____
_____
_____
_____

Who will you need to sell this idea to?

_____
_____
_____
_____
_____
_____
_____
_____
_____

Opportunity
1.   Describe your idea's viability by identifying and describing:

a)   Your Potential Market

_____
_____
_____
_____
_____
_____

b)   Customer Profile

_____
_____
_____
_____
_____
_____

c)   Potential Size or Impact on Society

_____
_____
_____
_____
_____
_____

d)   Competition - Direct, and Indirect

_____
_____
_____
_____
_____
_____

e) Methods of Implementation

_____
_____
_____
_____
_____
_____
_____

2. What do you see as the potential

(a) strengths
(b) weaknesses
(c) opportunities
(d) threats

for introducing this idea into the marketplace?

_____
_____
_____
_____
_____
_____
_____
_____
_____
_____
_____
_____
_____
_____
_____
_____

3. What additional information would you require in order to determine the market demand for your idea?

_____
_____
_____
_____
_____
_____
_____
_____

4,   (b) Based on your analysis of the potential market for your product or service, what do you see as the niche(s) that need to be exploited?

_____
_____
_____
_____
_____
_____
_____
_____

(b)   What is currently not being done, that if it were done, would enhance your contribution?

_____
_____
_____
_____
_____
_____
_____
_____

5.   What additional emerging opportunities do you foresee?

_____
_____
_____
_____
_____
_____
_____
_____

6.   What makes you think your customers will buy this?

_____
_____
_____
_____
_____
_____
_____
_____

Resources

1.   What human resources will you require in order to make this
      service concept work? (*Be certain to include all those persons,
      both inside and outside your organization, who can assist this
      process.*)

      _____
      _____
      _____
      _____
      _____
      _____
      _____
      _____
      _____
      _____
      _____
      _____

2.   (a)What financial resources will need to be committed
                  in order to ensure the effective transition to an
                  entrepreneurial unit?

                  _____
                  _____
                  _____
                  _____
                  _____
                  _____
                  _____

      (b)   Where will the funding come from?

                  _____
                  _____
                  _____
                  _____
                  _____
                  _____

      (c)   Can you find resourceful ways in which you can
                  achieve these transformations?

                  _____
                  _____
                  _____
                  _____
                  _____

_____
_____
_____

1.(a) What factors would represent success for your enterprise?

_____
_____
_____
_____
_____
_____
_____

(b)   What creative approaches do you need to embody in order to get the most out of your resources?

_____
_____
_____
_____
_____
_____
_____

(c)   What specific resources do you require to make this work?

_____
_____
_____
_____
_____
_____
_____

(d)   How will you obtain the needed resources?

_____
_____
_____
_____
_____
_____

Conclusions

Prepare a summary presentation of the above 'Creating Your Future: The Enterprise Diamond' exercise:

_____
_____
_____
_____
_____
_____
_____
_____
_____
_____
_____
_____
_____
_____
_____
_____
_____
_____
_____
_____
_____
_____
_____
_____
_____
_____
_____
_____
_____

Colleagues' Responses to Entreplexity® = Entrepreneurship + Complexity

LEVERAGING LEARNING INTO SUCCESS

Gene Luczkiw was a friend, mentor and inspiration for me in achieving a sense of personal harmony and order in the stress-filled and chaotic environment of government bureaucracy.

As a senior executive in a government department considered as the main "face" of government programs and services for Canadian citizens, it became a major struggle for me in my attempt to meet the general public's growing expectations for quality government programming within the often autocratic and restraining structures of a highly formed and limiting bureaucracy. Couple this with the requirement to "do more with less" philosophy and an ever-shrinking resource budget and you have a business model set up for failure.

I first became acquainted with Gene through our government's funding of "The New Enterprise Store," a business program dedicated to taking unemployed and troubled youth and teaching them how to find careers or molding them into successful budding entrepreneurs. This, I believe, was the start of Gene's formal transition from teacher to Master Educator. His boundless energy, commitment to making a difference in society and an infectious sense of humour made him a favourite amongst students, colleagues and community leaders alike.

The success of his first endeavour into teaching entrepreneurship evolved into the creation of many New Enterprise Stores throughout Ontario and Eastern Canada, teaching unemployed youth the ways and means of providing self-sufficiency and business success through entrepreneurship. He leveraged the learning gleaned from his students' successes and parlayed them into teachings and curricula for all members of society including business leaders, members of academia and government leaders, who were seeking ways to re-engineer outdated business models. Through these efforts and constant discussions, I, too, came to acquire Gene's ability to seek out new business paradigms on the edge of a government bureaucracy. It was through these lessons that I, too, was able to apply this knowledge to my own government department, transforming it into an entrepreneurial enterprise that became known as a "model" for government. By applying the concepts of an entrepreneurial enterprise, we received international recognition as well as being recognized by our community as one of the "Entrepreneurs of the Year" in 1998.

Gene continued to develop his understanding of entrepreneurial habits and behaviours by formally creating the Institute for Enterprise Education. Not only was he able to continue his work of changing societal views on creating successful enterprises on the edge of a chaotic global economy, but he was also able to influence those he felt could have the greatest impact on youth and their desire for rewarding careers - the education community. His teaching to secondary school and university educators started to change the paradigm in the way the academic community influenced the minds and educational direction of today's youth. Through instructing educators in the ways and means of enterprising habits and entrepreneurship, Gene was slowing having the desired effect of changing the learning paradigm for students from kindergarten to post secondary education.

His greatest legacy will be the many students, teachers and community leaders who went through his programs, who were influenced by his teachings and who continue to practice and live in the spirit of entrepreneurship.

Reading *Entreplexity® = Entrepreneurship + Complexity* is a fitting testament to Gene's work and provides a unique insight into what makes entrepreneurs tick, as well as how to engender one's own innate talents and abilities and leverage them into successful entrepreneurial habits and behaviours. Through the lessons learned and dedication to practice these traits, students will be on the leading edge of a new business paradigm, providing career and business opportunities well suited to the changes occurring in today's global marketplace.

Jim Williams
Senior Executive
Human Resources Development Canada (Retired)

PASSION, EXCITEMENT AND THE NEW ECONOMY

Gene was one of the most 'upbeat' persons I have ever met. He was passionate about his work, his family and his friends. This passion comes through in his writings. He viewed the new economy with excitement. In this book, you can see the holistic approach he took to analyze the qualities that were necessary for success as an entrepreneur in this changing world. As he says in his book, "a common element running through the research of successful entrepreneurs identifies the journey, rather than the destination, as the key motivator." This describes the way Gene approached life. I am honoured that I could share a small part of that journey with him.

Ken Atkinson
Lawyer & former Member of Parliament for St. Catharines
St. Catharines, Ontario
Canada

CONTINUING OUR QUEST FOR CREATIVITY, INNOVATION AND ENTREPRENEURSHIP

After reviewing "Entreplexity®= Entrepreneurship + Complexity", I realize all over again how much I miss Gene and his profound catalytic effect on my colleagues and myself.

I was already a healthy innovator before I met Gene. Like an addict, though, I was desperate for more innovation, the ultimate fix. Creativity is so powerful; how do we get more of it and from more of our people? How do we convert it into innovation?

When I first heard some of Gene's speech, I just had to plug in and get to know him. I needed to tap this loud animated source of inspiration.

Some of the initial attraction was like-minded thinking, but Gene was able to open up my eyes to "people potential" and "people understanding" that most simply don't know exists. Gene gave us a map to hidden treasure and future success.

The power and complexity of the human mind is actually hidden behind poor leadership, mental paradigms and weak wills. Gene's help to vision and see the potential led to believing in it, which, in turn, became a major step towards reaping the bounty.

To vision and believe Gene ensured we understood our brain, its power, and its differences. Before his intervention, we selfishly respected our own, while openly shunning human difference as if it was caused by genetic flaw. After Gene, we saw that difference was simply misunderstood complexity, in fact, diversification in human makeup and thinking was to be revered, collected and leveraged.

To this day, we continue our quest for creativity, innovation and entrepreneurship. Today, thanks to Gene, we are doing it as a team and "team" has morphed into "everyone in our company."

The really good news for readers of "Entreplexity®=Entrepreneurship + Complexity" is that while it is simply printed words, they are Gene's and have remotivated me. He is still here! Reading his mantra is a fix; it's so relevant, true and inspirational, especially in today's economic chaos.

Gene, again, I thank you!

Robert B. Magee
Chairman & CEO
The Woodbridge Group
Mississauga, Ontario
Canada

MEMORABLE MEETING

I first met Gene at one minute past three on the afternoon of Friday 9th September 1994 at the Institute for Enterprise in St Catharines, Ontario, and my first words to him were, 'I'm sorry we're a bit late, we've just travelled three thousand miles to meet you.' He laughed heartily at this and that got us off to a flyer.

A colleague and I had just spent a week in New Brunswick on a study visit to select examples of good practice in enterprise education that could be 'imported' to Scotland, as part of Scottish Enterprise's recently-launched Business Birth Rate Strategy. As our return flight from Halifax had to go via Toronto, our hosts recommended that we pay a visit to an enterprise guru with the unusual surname, Luczkiw.

For the rest of that Friday and all of Saturday, we learned so much about Gene that proves that first impressions are, indeed, extremely important and do, indeed, influence your long-term view of any individual. He was supercharged with enthusiasm and optimism, and he had that effect on everyone he came in contact with. Over a 24-hour period, we had a conducted tour of the major physical and cultural features of the Niagara area, visited two of the leading wineries where we bypassed the guides and met the owners, ate in two excellent restaurants, and attended a seminar for local entrepreneurs. You can tell a great deal about an individual by the way others react to meeting them, and in Gene's case, it was like they were greeting a long-lost brother.

At the business end of our visit, it was obvious that Gene had an encyclopaedic knowledge of entrepreneurship and the entrepreneurial process, and more importantly, an ability to get the message across in an easy-to-understand way, without sacrificing its intellectual concepts. In short, this was a guy we could do business with and six months later, he was the keynote speaker at a conference for Scotland's college principals at the Old Course Hotel in St Andrews, after which he was a regular visitor for the next five years, headlining major events, running CPD workshops, and working closely with specific clients, Scottish Enterprise and Kilmarnock College, in particular.

Gene was at his best when addressing an audience, and no matter how often you had heard the same story or anecdote, he had the knack of making it sound fresh every time. He possessed the charisma and zeal of a revivalist preacher, but this was no latter day Elmer Gantry, as he also backed up his hypotheses with an academic and intellectual rigour that could withstand any challenges. He was a prolific writer and his ability to switch seamlessly from the classical to the contemporary to illustrate a point, always kept the reader interested and motivated. He fully understood Karl Marx's quote that 'history repeats itself, first as tragedy, second as farce', but Gene took the optimistic view that the future could always be brighter than the past.

What is generally not appreciated by many who only saw Gene working an audience or leading a workshop, is that he was a first-rate researcher, which helps to explain the clarity of thought and expression in his ideas and presentations. He had the uncanny ability to distil complex theory and express it in easy-to-understand bite-size chunks.

My abiding memory of Gene is when I was sitting with him on the veranda of the Marine Hotel in Troon, Scotland in September 1996, overlooking the Firth of Clyde as the sun set over the Isle of Arran, listening to him as he postulated yet another of his big ideas on the new economic order, and I remember thinking, 'it doesn't get any better than this'. I consider myself blessed to have known Gene for what proved to be five exciting and fulfilling years, both personally and professionally, and I know that many people will join me in asking, 'when will we see his like again?'

Gordon McVie, BA (HONS), PGCE, is a graduate of Strathclyde University and a former geography teacher and college lecturer. He was Enterprise Education Manager at Scottish Enterprise/Careers Scotland from 1990 until his retirement in 2006. Since then he has been Outreach Co-ordinator in the Department of Electronic and Electrical Engineering at the University of Strathclyde. Gordon is a co-founder of the Scottish Space School and the creator and founder of the Global Enterprise Challenge.

It is apparent from reading Gene's book that the amount of research, interpretation, consideration, and evaluation that went into his product is absolutely 'mind-boggling', to coin a phrase. I have always known how pensive Gene was and what a voracious reader he was also. His publication is a font of information and provides connections to so many sources.

All in all, the book is a masterpiece of writing and clearly coveys the complex and creative thoughts and approaches that were so unique to Gene. He was certainly a genius when it came to bringing a myriad of information and research results to light and being able to apply these to current day applications.

Respectfully submitted,
Carol Bulmer
President
Evergreen Performance Management Ltd.
Toronto, Ontario
Canada

THE MOTIVATOR

I met Gene Luczkiw for the first time in May 2002, at the "Enterprise for Life Conference" in Nottingham, UK. He was presenting a speech "Instilling the Spirit of Enterprise in Nottinghamshire – Learning Strategies for the New Millennium". Since the organizer of the conference was a project partner of mine at that time, I got the opportunity to meet Gene before his presentation – a meeting that I will always remember for the rest of my life. From the first handshake, looking into his smiling, friendly and curious face, you instantly felt you were meeting your 'mate', and 'mate' he became and 'mate' he was, until he left us in October, 2008.

Gene's speech was fantastic. Not only was it an amazing and visionary global scan that gave us a totally fresh and enlightened lecture of the status of the enterprise world, but, in addition, Gene's energy, presence on the stage and body language gave the audience the experience that we were a part of his wonderful jamming jazz band metaphor. I felt that when Gene raised his arms and began to speak that he was like a conductor and I was one of his musicians. My inner clarinet started to play and I am sure that Gene could hear all the trombones, basses, trumpets, guitars and drums coming from the audience in this spectacular performance.

Travelling around Europe together with my project partners, Gene and his wonderful wife and 'soulmate', Jane, we searched for the very best answers on how to organize an Enterprise Learning Network. We were like a travelling jazz band for three years. Gene was the conductor; the inspiration and the motivator for us all. He made all our problems look like wonderful challenges and during these years, when he was present, he changed me from being a mediocre solo player to a first-class jam session player.

Gene was not only concerned with entrepreneurial factors and approaches concerning business development, but he was also very concerned about the development of the 'human being', 'the entrepreneur' and the development of people's entrepreneurial 'mindset'. I recall that his definition of enterprise was:

> "The taking of initiative to achieve a self-determined goal, that is part of a future vision; in order to achieve one's own meaning in life, while sharing its achievements with others in the community".

This was a wonderful approach to life and work and this became not only a personal slogan for me, but also a guiding star for me in my professional life.

Gene, like myself, was very concerned about how entrepreneurship and enterprise were going through a transition from an economic context to a pedagogic and educational context. We both discussed the fact that although entrepreneurship and enterprise have their etymological significance and epistemological argument in the economic context, they were being converted and implemented into pedagogic and educational context, and we wondered what kind of effect that would have on pedagogy and education, in general.

Our concern was that this transition process was being influenced by economic factors, politicians and governmental bodies who saw possibilities to start this economic pump-priming policy in schools, in order to educate young people to understand the concept of economic development earlier in life. However, the problem, in our view, was that when something is being transferred from one context to another, in this case, education, educators would need to be made aware of what makes up the best learning conditions needed to nurture entrepreneurial talents in their students, otherwise, we might be in danger of losing the perspective of personal growth and progress. Is it by giving pupils knowledge of how to start a business or is it by offering them learning concepts that stimulate all their entrepreneurial 'genes and fibers' so that they can accumulate the necessary knowledge and understanding of how to handle challenges and changes in society, in the marketplace and, also, in their personal daily life? Although we never got the opportunity to come to any definitive conclusion about our concerns, I have a very strong feeling that Gene's final message was built upon his definition of enterprise.

Another thing I remember was Gene's ability to summarize strategic steps into 'one word statements'. As is present in the book, he always used the 7 P's, as he called it, as a structure for strategic planning. Using the 7 P's, people can feel free to stake out their approach to their life and career in order to develop strategic projects of any sort. Gene's 7 P's became a guide for us:

1. Develop *Perspective* - how to get an overview, among other things – to learn one's history.
2. *Possibilities* – to develop your mission, vision and strategies.
3. We constantly need to interact with *People* - by learning about ourselves and others, we grow.
4. When we are *Passionate* when we develop self-awareness, thus developing our creativity.
5. We all need to develop a *Purpose* by searching for our core beliefs and values.
6. We *Perform* by developing our talents and ideas and by looking for opportunities and resources, we start to grow.
7. Perhaps the most important and one that we sometimes forget is being constantly aware of the *Progress* of our life, by using milestone evaluation and planning in order to keep control of it.

The reflection, understanding and insight that lies within the framework of the 7 P's, constitutes, in many ways, the big difference between success and failure. The only thing I miss in this framework of strategic awareness is the 8th P, *Persistence,* which for me is about courage - having the courage to take risks and having the patience to look for the best result. All of these P's are both powerful analyzing and planning instruments, but also are reflection instruments. They allow us to think out of the box and boost our creative energy. Last, but not least, instead of searching for fixed answers, you are inspired to search for more insight and knowledge by asking new questions.

Gene always asked good questions which led to good discussions. He did not search for the ultimate answers but, instead, he always searched for the answer beyond the preliminary answers. An answer for him seemed to be a stepping stone for new questions. Gene was an inspiration for all of us as a role model. He showed us how to inspire people to have the motivation and strength to be like Asterope, stimulating us to believe that we can make our light shine the other way with an endless array of possibilities.

Dag Ofstad
Centre For Practical Knowledge, Department Of Professional Studies,
Nordland University
Bodø, Norway

EMBEDDED ENTERPRISE EDUCATION

In 2008, the White Rose Centre for Enterprise at the University of Sheffield, hosted a workshop on enterprise education. The structure of the workshop was informality, with soapbox presentations where individuals could present their points of view and showcase their work, which would then generate comment and discussion. At the end of the day, the themes and presentations were pulled together by Alan Gibb. In order to have an international viewpoint, Gene was invited to the workshop, but ill health prevented him from being present. Through a very shaky video link, we were able to have Gene's views on the workshop discussion and for some of us, an initial exposure to his work on Entreplexity®. Gene's views and approach were not diminished by the shaky video link, and provided us with a wider view of the somewhat Anglo-focused presentations and discussion that had taken place that day. His was a thought-provoking contribution, which led to further dialogue and debate in the evening.

To have Gene's ideas brought together in this volume is of immense value, given the current climate in terms of the economy and education. One is struck by how fresh and relevant Gene's ideas and writing are – and yet his work is at least five years old. The world has changed vastly in the last five + years. And prophetic; he foresaw many developments, not least that of Apple with Steve Jobs back in the role of CEO. This brings to mind two points: what would Gene be expounding now, and how the speed of development in enterprise and entrepreneurship education is relatively slow.

Here at Sheffield, our focus is on embedded enterprise education. Under Theme 8 Innovation, Gene shows the need as educational: 'What's required are educational systems that teach and motivate students to learn and to be creative, rather than recall information. Governments and regulatory frameworks must help to liberate the human spirit for invention and creation, rather than acting as a bureaucratic brake on change and breakthrough' (Tapscott, *The Digital Economy*). Over the last five years, the reverse has been true, with education being subjected to ever more regulation. The liberation of the human spirit for invention and creation in Higher Education must come through enterprise being embedded in the curriculum, where students get to understand the value of their academic learning, by applying it to 'real' situations to the benefit of the students on many levels, not least, their own self-efficacy; the academic, the university and the wider community, as a whole. While economic change is encouraging action and acceptance, and there is a hierarchical will to embrace enterprise embedded in the curriculum, there is still much to do. The students' enterprise learning is encapsulated in Czikszentmihalyi's flow experience – they work longer, harder and gain more satisfaction than from standard methods of academic learning.

So how could Entreplexity® work within the curriculum? Certainly, embedded enterprise modules work best 'on the edge of existing structures (modules)'. Perhaps, we need to encourage students to 'create a personal vision that is consistent with their meaning and purpose on the one hand and aligned with the leaders on the other', as part of their embedded enterprise module. The leader 'needs to enunciate a compelling vision that engages every participant in the enterprise...' – this interconnectedness allows the leader (the academic) and the students to collaborate and evolve in ways that cannot be encompassed in the standard learning framework. This could happen by embracing Entreplexity® in the curriculum as a way forward.

Finally, the quote from Samuelsohn seems to have particular resonance: "We have yet to see any benefits to business brought about by over 1,000,000 MBA's." We are in a period of change and instability which cannot be addressed by the MBA Model of Business. Let's see what Entreplexity® can do.

Elena Rodriguez Falcon
Director of Enterprise Education
University of Sheffield
&
Jenny Moore
Enterprise Learning Coordinator
University of Sheffield
Sheffield, England

REMEMBERING GENE LUCZKIW

I first met Gene in the early 1990's when the Vintner's Quality Alliance (VQA), the newly vinted premium wine industry and Henry of Pelham Family Estate Winery were all in their infancyI too was young and excited and somewhere in my 20's. It was a once in a lifetime opportunity in our industry as we were transforming from a low quality, highly protected business to a high quality, completely open market that the "Free Trade Deal" from the late 80's with the United States brought on. Wineries that had survived and prospered for decades were consolidating or going out of business, while at the same time very small, high quality estate wineries often working together were opening up; all of this happening in the grip of a national recession and the gutting of the industrial base in the Niagara Peninsula.

Gene recognized the re birth of the wine industry and considered it a remarkable business occurrence and became fascinated with the wineries and most importantly the people involved. He conducted a number of studies to show what and why it was happening and most encouraging to those of us in the middle of it, that it would be successful. That is what I remember the most about Gene. His unquenchable enthusiasm for people and an overall positive outlook on the world. Every time I met with Gene he gave me books to read. My three favorite are the E-myth by Michael Gerber, Built to Last by Jim Collins and Jerry Porras and a few Peter Drucker books. Our meetings were long, loud and expressive with hands flinging throughout the air.

Not everyone understood Gene, but my brothers and I did. At a time when Henry of Pelham was growing fast and moving from a very small company to a small to mid - sized winery we realized we needed to get some help reorganizing the entire company, restructuring everyone's job descriptions, formalize what they did and who they reported to and in some cases change job descriptions altogether. A big task for 3 liberal arts majors. With Gene's help for 2 years in a row we did some sessions that helped us as owner/operators focus our ideas and worked with the staff to help them understand how and why we needed to change the way we operating as a team. A process that often has many employees leaving companies because they believe that management has changed for the negative under the pressure of growth and opportunity. What could have been a nightmare turned into a very positive time for Henry of Pelham and we did not lose one employee through the process. Many are still with us today and we are significantly larger now. They also commented specifically on Gene's talent, unbridled enthusiasm and his general love for people and humanity. His belief that entrepreneurship can be taught, while at times debatable, is none the less a worthwhile and intriguing discussion for business people and our learning institutions to consider. I miss Gene and am very glad his life's work has been documented for everyone to remember and learn from.

Paul Speck
President
Henry of Pelham Family Estate Winery
St. Catharines, Ontario
Canada
May, 2012

NOTES

[1] M. Mitchell Waldrop, Complexity, The Emerging Science at the Edge of Order and Chaos, (Simon & Schuster, New York, 1992), p. 17.

[2] Paul Rohmer, Thought Leaders, Joel Kurtzman, Editor, Booz-Allen & Hamilton (Jossey-Bass, San Francisco, 1998), p.68

[3] Gerald Ross, Michael Kay, Toppling the Pyramids, (Times Books, 1994), p. 30.

[4] Ibid, p 255.

[5] Kevin Kelly, The New Rules of the New Economy, *Wired Magazine*, September 1997, p. 194

[6] Gene Luczkiw, The Institute for Enterprise Education, February, 1999

[7] Donald Tapscott, The Digital Economy, (McGraw Hill, 1996), p. 53.

[8] Ibid

[9] Ibid, p. 55.

[10] Ibid, p.62

[11] Ibid, p. 65.

[12] Ibid, p. 67.

[13] Ibid, p. 66.

[14] Richard Dawkins, Evolution of Consciousness, From Gaia to Selfish Gene, edited by Connie Barlow, (MIT Press, Cambridge, MA), p 219.

[15] *Descartes' Error: Emotion, Reason, and the Human Brain*, Putnam, 1994; revised Penguin edition, 2005

[16] Richard C. Lewontin, Not In Our Genes, p. 189. From Gaia to Selfish Gene, Connie Barlow, 1944, MIT Press.
[17] Ibid, p. 31
[18] Ibid, p. 34.
[19] Ibid, p. 199.
[20] Ibid, p. 18.
[21] Viktor E. Frankl, Man's Search for Meaning, p 111.
[22] Ibid, p 113.

CPSIA information can be obtained at www.ICGtesting.com
Printed in the USA
BVOW011232290113

311869BV00002B/45/P

9 789462 090620